Anthropology of Contemporary Issues

A SERIES EDITED BY

ROGER SANJEK

[ii]

Civilized Women

GENDER AND PRESTIGE IN SOUTHEASTERN LIBERIA

Mary H. Moran

Cornell University Press

Ithaca and London

First published 1990 by Cornell University Press.

International Standard Book Number 0-8014-2293-0 (cloth)
International Standard Book Number 0-8014-9554-7 (paper)
Library of Congress Catalog Card Number 89-22398
Printed in the United States of America
Librarians: Library of Congress cataloging information
appears on the last page of the book.

⊖ The paper used in this publication meets the minimum requirements of the American National Standard for Permanence of Paper for Printed Library Materials Z39.48–1984.

For Jordy

Contents

Illustrations, Figures, Tables

Illustrations

Figures

Tables

Preface

Since 1974, when Michelle Rosaldo and Louise Lamphere first set the agenda for feminist anthropology, much debate has centered on how to conceptualize status differences between women and men. Early arguments focused on whether status asymmetry by gender was a human universal (Leacock 1978; Sacks 1979; Rogers 1978), on how to separate biological from psycho-sociocultural explanations for inequality (Rosaldo 1974, 1980; Chodorow 1974; Ortner 1974), and on recording the details of women's lives, previously ignored (Weiner 1976; Goodale 1971; Wolf 1972, among others). Out of this decade and a half of research and writing have come a number of theoretical paradigms, several of which, as will be obvious to the reader, have greatly influenced my presentation of the material in this book.

Civilized Women is an anthropological study of the connections between cultural constructions of gender and other means of social ranking, based on fifteen months of fieldwork in Liberia, a small nation in West Africa. Liberia has long presented analysts with perplexing contradictions. It is Africa's oldest independent, black-ruled republic, yet for its entire history it has been at the mercy of foreign powers, prevented by massive debts and the fear of colonial annexation from defining its own course in the world. Liberia was founded in 1822 for African-American settlers fleeing racial intolerance in the United States, yet as late as 1930 the League of Nations accused the Liberian government of profiting from the forcible recruitment of indigenous labor for export to the Spanish colony of Fernando Po. Finally, in an area of West Africa characterized by small-scale, relatively egalitarian societies, the Liberian state was, until the military coup of 1980, founded on a castelike division between a settler-descended or "repatriate" elite (see Dunn and Tarr 1988 for a discussion of the replacement of the older term *Americo-Liberian* with *repatriate*) and the bulk of the indigenous population.

Although class differences and variations in education and background were evident in other West African nations during the nineteenth century, the case of Liberia appears to be unique. D. Elwood Dunn and S. Byron Tarr have suggested that the source of this uniqueness lies in Liberia's nineteenth-century roots as a philanthropic experiment in colonization and independence. "Unlike the rest of Africa then, with experience of popular movements against colonialism and unlike the post-war era in Africa when socialist and egalitarian ideologies were seen as an appropriate motor force moving new nations, Liberia's background lies in the nineteenth century" (1988:43–44). In the following pages, that nineteenth-century background and its implications for the present will be explored in greater detail.

Although other areas of West Africa also experienced the return of African-American repatriates, only in Liberia and Sierra Leone were these populations both sufficiently large and supported by a European presence to remain discrete from the surrounding indigenous people. The social status division of the Liberian population has been portrayed by the elite as based on rigid genealogical lines, but the barrier was, in practice, more permeable than might be supposed. The repatriate elite in fact incorporated numbers of native Liberians through institutions such as wardship, apprenticeship, informal polygyny, and political patronage, thereby bridging the two sectors of Liberian society with an intricate web of personal ties and allegiances. But neither personal ties nor the 1980 military coup have fundamentally altered the deep status divisions in Liberian society. Prestige of occupation and social connections continue to count more toward an individual's status than does actual wealth and are usually viewed as the means to, rather than the result of, a personal fortune. J. Gus Liebenow has accurately described Liberian political and social history as "the evolution of privilege" (1969).

[xii]

Over more than two hundred years, this national prestige system has become incorporated by the numerous ethnic groups living within Liberia's borders. The different manifestations of this process have been conditioned by localized sequences of repatriate settlement, missionization, and migration of wage labor. In addition, Liberian ethnic groups have integrated national-level status systems with their own evaluations of relative worth, including the prestige differences accorded to men and women. The implications of the convergence of these status and gender systems for the Glebo women of Cape Palmas, in southeastern Liberia, are the subject of this book.

My approach focuses on the intersection of cultural constructions of gender with other systems of ranking among the Glebo. I take an actor-centered approach, emphasizing both the constraining nature of prestige categories, including gender, on their occupants and the negotiation and management of these constraints by individuals. It is in this process of everyday management, what Sherry B. Ortner (1984) refers to as "practice," that both the reproduction of the system and its potential for change are located. Through a close analysis of household composition, economic activities, and ritual events in the Glebo community, I show how different prestige systems, including gender, mutually construct and define one another.

Much of my graduate training at Brown University, as well as the fifteen months of fieldwork for this book, were supported by a National Science Foundation Graduate Fellowship. Additional funding came from my undergraduate institution, Mount Holyoke College, in the form of a Hannum-Warner Alumnae Travel Grant. Both institutions have my gratitude for making the research remarkably worry-free financially. Before leaving for Liberia, I was fortunate to receive valuable advice and field contacts from Jane Martin, Jo Sullivan, and Svend Holsoe; through them, I met some of my closest Liberian friends. I gratefully acknowledge the assistance of the Institute of Research at the University of Liberia and of the many administrators, faculty, and staff for their help, hospitality, and friendship. In particular, Magdalene David and Joyce Mends-Cole shared with me their intense interest in the role of Liberian women in national life. In many stimulating conversations, they helped me to focus my thinking beyond the immediate experience of fieldwork.

I must also acknowledge the cooperation and support of another Liberian institution, the W. V. S. Tubman College of Technology in Cape Palmas, where I held the position of visiting instructor. This affiliation with the college allowed me to extend my stay in Liberia by five months. Among the many Glebo, Nyabo, and other Grebo- and Kru-speaking people among whom I lived, I am proud to acknowledge Samuel Yede Wallace, Glebo historian and linguist, and my census assistants, Sarah Y. Howe and Beatrice Hodge Proud. They, with my foster family in Hoffman Station, the Reverend and Mrs. William Sodo Newton and their household, have my thanks and affection and are often in my thoughts. The congregations of numerous Cape Palmas churches were always tolerant of the stranger who attended their services, meetings, and funerals. A great many other organizations and people have contributed to this project, and I owe a debt of gratitude to each of them.

I have been fortunate in belonging to a generation of women anthropologists who entered the field after others had already established the legitimacy of feminist research, often at some cost to their own professional careers. I have been privileged to work closely with some of these pioneers. Once fieldwork was completed, the masses of data were shaped into an argument with the invaluable help of Louise Lamphere, for many years a mentor, friend, and role model as well as an inspiring and demanding teacher. Kay B. Warren, my first model as an anthropologist, scholar, and feminist, also contributed greatly as an insightful reader, continuing an interest in my career begun in my undergraduate days. That I am an anthropologist today is largely a result of her example. Philip Leis and William O. Beeman also provided rigorous, helpful readings and comments.

I thank the editors and reviewers for Cornell University Press, especially Peter Agree, Roger Sanjek, and Warren d'Azevedo, for their helpful advice and encouragement. Revision and polishing of the manuscript were accomplished with the help of a Junior Faculty Leave and a supplementary grant from the Faculty Research Council of Colgate University. I am grateful for the support and encouragement of my colleagues in the Department of Sociology and

Anthropology at Colgate. I could not ask for a better working environment. An appointment at Brown University as a visiting scholar in anthropology for 1988–89 provided access to library and other resources vital to the completion of the project. I am grateful also for the artistic talents of Imogene Lim and Alan Leveillee and for the careful editorial work of Trudie Calvert and Roger Haydon. I must acknowledge the International African Institute, the Longman Group of publishers, and the editorial board of the *Liberian Studies Journal* for permission to reprint some maps.

Finally, I thank my husband, Jordan E. Kerber, for his love, care, support, and friendship. He has suffered through long separations, processed my film, managed my finances, nursed me through malaria, been a computer consultant, proofreader, editor, and unfailing partner in a dual-career household. In his own scholarly career, he has provided an example of efficiency, determination, and intellectual integrity. He has been the one constant in the long process leading to this book, and for that reason and many others, it is dedicated to him.

MARY H. MORAN

Providence, Rhode Island

Civilized Women

[1]

Conceptualizing Gender
and Prestige

At first glance it would appear that, of all the Liberian ethnic groups, the Glebo are a poor choice for a study of status and prestige because they have no tradition of ranked lineages or aristocratic families. Politically, they are a nonstate people, organizing into small, autonomous communities and recognizing only loose, nonbinding alliances with other towns. One nineteenth-century American missionary characterized Glebo political structure as "the purest of democracies" (John Payne, quoted in Martin 1968:15). Although this evaluation was not entirely accurate, it does seem clear that most Glebo status distinctions were made on the basis of gender and age until the arrival of African-American settlers and Christian missionaries in the Cape Palmas region in 1834.

The very lack of elaborate status differentiation among the Glebo, however, provides a point from which to examine both historical change and the present situation. Like other Liberians, the Glebo of today recognize a difference between unschooled subsistence agriculturalists and Western-educated, literate wage earners. This two-part model of cultural difference, originally conceived as the contrast between European coastal traders and indigenous Africans, was applied also to the African-American settlers and later expanded to include a class of mission-educated natives who had adopted a lifestyle based on a recognizably Western model (Brown 1982; Fraenkel 1964, 1966; Martin 1968; Tonkin 1981). This Western-style mode of life is designated in the local folk idiom as "civilized," a term that disturbs anthropologists but is used unselfconsciously throughout Liberia. In Monrovia and some other settler communities, people in this category usually attempted to "pass" into the repatriate elite, cutting official ties with their "tribal" relatives and adopting English names and invented genealogies. Although this practice has ended in recent decades and especially since the 1980 military coup, it was common even into the 1950s (Fraenkel 1964).

The situation on the southeast coast, where this study focuses, is quite different. The influence of missions appears to have been greater than that of the settlers on the indigenous Kru- and Grebo-speaking peoples. In this region, the early rise of a "civilized native" or "mission" community created a basic division among people who continued to regard themselves primarily as members of indigenous groups. Unable or unwilling to assimilate to the repatriate elite and barred from traditional political and ritual offices by their new religion, the civilized southeasterners made a place for themselves as wage workers and lower-level bureaucrats in the Liberian national society while maintaining strong town, clan, and lineage identities and ties with their tribal origins.

Linguistically, this group of people is designated by the English terms *civilized* or *mission* in the southeastern region (Glebo: *mesa*, mission, and *kobo de*, civilized life, to live in the European manner, Innes 1967:53). The Kru word *kui* or *kwi*, which has entered Liberian English and is used nationally to denote *civilization*, is rarely heard among the Glebo. The opposite of *civilized* is *country*, *tribal*, or *native*, the last term being most frequently used in Cape Palmas (Glebo: *bli*, country, and *wodopee*, town person, which Innes defines as "uncivilized, a person unfamiliar with western culture"; ibid.:124). Elizabeth Tonkin notes that there is a pejorative connotation to the terms *native* or *country:* "Most terms opposed to *kwi* are not neutral but denigratory." She believes, however, that Euro-American observers have incorrectly reified an opposition that "is a means of counterpointing experiences which in reality can be shared by the same person. . . . *Kwi* and *Zo* (a term used to designate an indigenous ritual specialist in northwestern Liberia) are not really binary oppositions but identify different domains of knowledge, power, and expertise" (1981:322). I will argue that the Glebo have created their own model of civilization apart

[2]

from that provided by the local repatriate community (for a similar argument, see Tonkin on the Kru of the town of Siklipo, ibid.:316). Civilization, for the Glebo, came to represent an alternative path to individual success, based on standards set outside the village community and firmly linked to the regional and international politico-economic system developing along the West African coast in the nineteenth century. Throughout this book, I will use the contrastive pair civilized/native to refer to this important and long-standing status division in Glebo and Liberian national society.

What is most striking about the centrality of this concept in Liberia is its absence in other parts of coastal West Africa. Although most of the continent was subjected to the "civilizing mission" of European colonialism, rarely has this resulted in a distinct and highly elaborated status category. In Chapter 3, I compare the Liberian situation with that of the rest of West Africa in greater detail, but it is important to keep in mind that the concept developed within a unique political context of repatriate settlement and early independence.

Most Glebo seem to believe that civilized status is worth striving to attain, if not for oneself, then for one's children. For over a century in Liberia, literacy has been seen as the key to professional office jobs and a life of ease as compared with the arduous work of subsistence or commercial agriculture. Tonkin found that in a series of essays on the meaning of the word *kwi*, written by Jlao Kru students in Sasstown, the concept was "identified with the ways of whites, use of machines, with hygienic habits and rejection of superstition, and above all with wisdom and knowledge, more skilled and intelligent behavior" (1981:322).

Although, as Tonkin notes, "Every commentator on Liberia this century has mentioned these words (civilized/native) and thought them salient" (ibid.:305), never to my knowledge have they been discussed in relation to the equally important social division of the community by gender. Glebo women achieve civilized status in much the same manner as men, through formal education and training, yet they remain almost totally economically dependent on male wage earners. Being civilized severely constrains a woman's ability to support herself by limiting her to economic activities in which she must compete (often unequally) with men. Men have the

[3]

advantage, on the whole, of higher levels of education because parents are usually more willing to invest in the schooling of sons than of daughters. A common rationale offered for the preference for educating boys is that they cannot "spoil themselves" with early pregnancies, thereby wasting their parents' investment. Unlike the other counties in Liberia, girls in Maryland County, where this study focuses, are not allowed to return to public and mission schools once they have borne a child, although they may finish their educations at private night schools. In any case, Liberian men tend to be more qualified for jobs in the wage sector than are women (see Carter and Mends-Cole 1982:149 for 1980 Liberian education statistics) and are more likely to be hired by bureaucracies patterned after the sex-segregated occupational systems of the West.

Ideally a civilized woman should resemble a Western-style housewife, but there are contradictions between the ideal and actual lives of civilized women that appear more crucial for their overall prestige than that of men. I would argue that, although often economically dependent, the civilized Glebo women of Cape Palmas are anything but ladies of leisure. They work very hard at the domestic tasks required by large, complex households and frequently find themselves desperately short of assistance and of ready cash. Furthermore, their claim to civilized status is tenuous, depending both on their daily public behavior and on the financial situations of their husbands, lovers, and fathers. This is the key difference in the way the term *civilized* is applied to women and men. Men acquire civilized status for life, and though they may experience downward social and economic mobility through unemployment, alcoholism, or criminal behavior, they do not return to the status of natives. An unemployed civilized man, or a male high school or college student pursuing his education, has the option of forming a relationship with an economically active native woman with no loss of status on his part. Such a relationship does not provide a corresponding rise in the status of the woman. Native women, usually marketeers, seem willing to support civilized lovers in expectation of later sharing in their wages or, at the very least, securing civilized status for any children that might result from the union. These relationships are very often impermanent and not formalized by statutory marriage because ambitious men will need civilized wives later on in their careers. The children, however, are likely to be raised and educated in their father's civilized household, if and when he establishes one.

I am unaware of any instances in which a civilized woman entered into a marital or extramarital relationship with a native man. It is likely that, if such a case did occur, the woman's status would quickly slip to that of her "husband," especially if she took up the agricultural work a native man expects of his wife. Clandestine relationships are certainly possible, but I heard no current gossip or past accounts of such situations. In contrast, there are a large number of unions between civilized men and native women, many of whom are the nonresident second and third wives of high-status men.

Civilized women lose prestige by engaging in the "wrong" types of work, such as subsistence farming or marketing. "She used to be civilized" is frequently heard to describe a literate woman who has been forced by economic necessity to "tie lappa and make market," giving up the most visible symbol of civilized womanhood, the Western-style dress. The depth of feeling this loss of status evokes and the value accorded to civilization were expressed to me by one woman, who, in the process of describing her devotion to her children, claimed tearfully that she would "go in the market, never wear dresses again" if this were the only way she could keep her children in school—in other words, assure civilized status and the right to wear dresses for her daughters.

It hardly seems accidental that those areas of the economy which are off-limits to civilized women are precisely those associated with the work of native women according to the traditional Glebo division of labor. Marketing and subsistence farming are activities in which both civilized and native men, as well as civilized women, do not engage. These are also activities which are tightly bound up with the indigenous construction of women as providers, feeders, and sustainers of the household. Since civilized women should not participate in these productive activities, it is the reproductive side of their domestic labor which is stressed, with great emphasis given to housekeeping and training children in the civilized way of life. In practical terms, a state of economic dependency, unusual for other Glebo women, is produced and maintained by specific bans on

[5]

Illustration 1. A civilized Glebo woman shelling beans behind her house, Hoffman Station, 1983.

[6]

areas women have historically controlled. The exclusion from subsistence agriculture creates a dependence on cash wages or gifts for survival, while restrictions on public marketing eliminate the most obvious source of business opportunity for women with very little capital. Current high levels of unemployment and the general economic depression of the Cape Palmas area have made the competition for wage work extremely fierce, at the same time causing an exodus of young civilized men and women to Monrovia and other more favored areas of Liberia.

Among those who have stayed in Cape Palmas, the most obvious route for a civilized woman is marriage or a long-term relationship with a wage-earning civilized man. During the various periods of economic expansion which Cape Palmas has experienced since the 1830s, this was probably a more common solution than today. When professional work was available and men saw themselves as upwardly mobile within the local economy, having a civilized wife was a further marker of status, necessary for entertaining visitors, training children, and other "family status production" work (Papanek 1979:775). In other words, women's activities in the home complemented men's positions within the national and local systems of ranking. At present, with the southeast the most economically depressed and underdeveloped (in terms of infrastructure) region in Liberia, many civilized men are unemployed, or employed by a government (as teachers, clerks, public works officers, and the like) that often has difficulty meeting its payroll.

For this reason and others, I argue that the civilized/native distinction is not now (if it ever was) a *class* division in the usual sense of that term (for an opposing view, see Brown 1982). Although civilized and native Glebo stand in very different relationships to productive modes, their relationship to each other is not one that might lead to class conflict. Differences in wealth do not fall simply along status lines. At present, a native household in which subsistence needs are met by the woman's rice farm and which also produces a cash crop (such as sugarcane, which can be processed into liquor) undoubtedly receives a higher (and more reliable) income than does a civilized household headed by a male teacher and his less economically active wife. Although many civilized men continue to form sexual relationships with civilized women and to

[7]

father their children, they are less willing and able to contract formal marriages or even live-in arrangements and to contribute fully to the support of the household.

Such a situation leaves civilized women with few alternatives; giving up civilized status for farming or marketing is viewed less as a choice than as a desperate last resort. Civilized women often find themselves struggling both to uphold their status and to feed, clothe, and educate their children. A few, with professional jobs in nursing or teaching, are independent household heads with dependents of their own; more likely, such women become secondary wives to well-off civilized men who are already legally married. In other cases, a variety of strategies from nonpublic marketing to the careful manipulation of kin and friendship networks (including both native and civilized kin and friends), associational memberships, and relationships of fosterage, allow a single civilized woman and her household to "scrape by" without male support.

In this book, I will demonstrate that a contradiction exists between the cultural construction of civilized life as one of ease, wealth, and security and the economically insecure and socially tenuous reality of civilized women's lives. If, as will be demonstrated, native women have not only more secure economic bases in marketing and farming and independent sources of prestige within the native towns, why is this contradiction not evident to the Glebo? In moving from the larger theoretical issue of the intersection of gender with other systems of prestige to the specific Glebo material, the question becomes one of *why* would any woman *want* to be civilized? Why are there so many eager recruits for education and civilized training, and why do women struggle so valiantly to hold onto their status in the absence of a regular income? These questions will be taken up in the coming chapters.

I first became aware of the importance of the civilized/native distinction in Glebo society through a series of embarrassing (for the Glebo as well as for myself) faux pas in which I asked about the status of various individuals. The questions were inappropriate because I, as an obviously civilized, educated person, was expected immediately to recognize the signs of civilization (or lack thereof) in others and act accordingly. While at a funeral dance for a prominent civilized man, I once asked why the deceased's wife was not sitting with the other women of the family under the small "spirit house," which takes the place of the body at the ceremony. After much obvious embarrassment and discomfort, I received an answer: "Because she is civilized." The widow was then pointed out to me, seated with other civilized people in a special section of the audience. Although I was praised by both civilized and native Glebo for my efforts to learn the language and for my interest in "country custom," my initial inability to make this crucial social distinction aroused something akin to disbelief. I believe this response from the Glebo supports my contention that these categories are, indeed, Glebo constructions rather than my own.

But how can we conceptualize the intersection of these status constructions with Glebo ideas about men and women? Feminist research and scholarship have provided us with powerful models of gender as a culturally constituted status more all-pervasive than any other. Sherry Ortner and Harriet Whitehead, in laying out the framework for their study of gender and sexuality, suggest that we begin by focusing on these areas as "cultural (symbolic) constructs, and inquiring into the sources, processes, and consequences of their construction and organization" (1981:1). Gender is seen here as a system of meanings, attached to males and females, by which they gain cultural identities as men and women. The term *construct* or *construction* refers to the active way in which men and women imbue objects and concepts with meaning and use the resulting symbols both to order their social world and to constrain behavior within it. The immense cross-cultural variation of these gender constructions has long been recognized and remarked upon in anthropology, at least since the publication of Margaret Mead's *Sex and Temperament* in 1935.

Although simply describing the wide variation in the content of gender constructions may serve as a useful reminder that "natural processes of sex and reproduction furnish only a suggestive and ambiguous backdrop to the cultural organization of gender and sexuality" (Ortner and Whitehead 1981:1), I contend that the one universal characteristic of such systems is their asymmetrical nature (see Rosaldo 1980 for a statement of this position within the feminist debate). Although the degree of asymmetry between men and women is likewise variable, in all known cases, men and men's

[9]

activities are accorded the greatest social value. Also, men may legitimately contract agreements with other men transferring productive, reproductive, and sexual rights in adult women; the reverse situation is not known to exist (Lévi-Strauss 1969; Rubin 1975). This political and economic aspect of gender constructions must therefore inform any analysis of their specific symbolic expression in any one society.

One way in which political and economic factors may be incorporated into an analysis of gender is through the notion of cultural constraints. Ortner has described the movement from classical symbolic anthropology to a "practice" approach as a shift in emphasis "from what culture allows and enables people to see, feel, and do, to what it restricts and inhibits them from seeing, feeling, and doing. Further, although it is agreed that culture powerfully constitutes the reality that actors live in, this reality is looked upon with critical eyes: why this one and not some other? And what sorts of alternatives are people being dis-abled from seeing?" (1984:152). Among these alternatives, of course, are particular economic and political choices which cultural constraints relegate to the category of nonchoices.

Ortner locates the activity of constraint, therefore, in "the system," the cultural definitions of the world held by actors. She notes, however, that for many authors coming from a Marxist perspective, "while accepting the view of culture as powerfully constraining, they argue that hegemony is always more fragile than it appears." In other words, if cultures were entirely efficient in constraining actors' behavior to predetermined categories, there could be no possibility of historical change. The actor, who both constitutes the social reality and acts within it, must be brought back into the analysis. Thus Ortner sees the practice approach as positing "that society is a system, that the system is powerfully constraining, and yet that the system can be made and unmade through human action and interaction" (ibid.:153–54, 159). I prefer the word *constrains* to other, more causal terms (e.g., *determines*) simply because it implies this active component, a flexibility of choice, although within limits. Or, as Clifford Geertz has put it, "Culture orders action not by determining it but by providing the forms in terms of which it determines itself" (1965:203).

Ortner admits that her work is deeply influenced, through

Geertz, by Max Weber, and this influence is apparent in her and Whitehead's approach to gender. Gender is defined as "first and foremost a prestige structure" (1981:16). An analytical distinction is made between the relative value assigned to men and women and such factors as the sexual division of labor, differential control over resources, or the enforcement of one person's will over another (the Weberian definition of power, 1947:152). In the same way, Weber himself distinguishes between "social honor," or prestige, and other forms of political and economic power (i.e., class), claiming that the latter may be based on the former, but not vice versa (1946:180). In Chapter 3, I will show that the Glebo conception of civilization is remarkably consistent with Weber's definition of status honor.

"Prestige structures," in Ortner and Whitehead's terms, would seem to correspond to Ralph Linton's "patterns of reciprocal behavior," in which each separate status represents a polar position. But while "*A status,* in the abstract, is a position in a particular pattern . . . *the status* of any individual means the sum total of all the statuses which he occupies" (1936:113). The status of an individual, therefore, is roughly synonymous with that person's prestige or standing in the community. Weber used the term in this sense when he defined social status as "a typically effective claim to a positive or negative privilege with respect to social prestige" (1947:428). Prestige is often a relative and shifting level of evaluation, a complex negotiation between an individual's aspirations and assertions and the collective opinion of the community. Gender is often viewed as a status, immutable and ascribed at birth except in those rare societies that recognize intermediate or alternative categories of males and females (Whitehead 1981; Kirkpatrick 1980). Ortner and Whitehead suggest, however, that "prestige structures in any society tend toward symbolic consistency with one another" (1981:16). This means that gender constructions often inform other status distinctions and even provide a model for the organization of status categories occupied primarily or exclusively by men (Strathern, 1981). The Glebo, for whom relative age is a crucial mechanism for the allocation of prestige, neatly illustrate this point by collapsing age and gender hierarchies in the convenient formulation "men are always older than women."

Individual prestige, therefore, refers to the total complex of statuses held by a person in a particular community, taking into account the intersection of numerous statuses from numerous hierarchical systems, all of which are symbolically related to each other. Civilization, as a key marker of prestige for the Glebo, is both *a* status and *the* status of particular people who hold a constellation of others, including occupation, education, residence, church membership, and family of origin. When someone attains the status of a civilized person, he or she is both accorded prestige and constrained by the limits placed on the role that accompanies this position. As individuals strive to manage or manipulate their relative prestige, it becomes important to notice how gender constructions are also managed, invoked or ignored, challenged or reinforced.

Once gender is understood in this way, it can be seen as systematically related to other prestige hierarchies and inequalities within the same society: "A model adequate to understanding gender is then, we suggest, a model showing the connections between productive relationships, political processes, and folk conceptions of human nature" (Collier and Rosaldo 1981:277). Jane Collier and Michelle Rosaldo go beyond Ortner and Whitehead, who emphasize the symbolic aspect of gender constructions, to a view of gender as both grounded in and generated by human interaction, or practice, in a material world. Kay B. Warren has contrasted the symbolic position that cultural constructs determine (and therefore explain) human behavior with the more grounded approach, which sees gender as "a product of on-going social/political/economic negotiations, not just a set of conceptual categories. Note that both approaches are concerned with cultural meanings. One sees meaning as captured in native categories, the other in the social and political processes of daily life" (1983:13–14).

For the analysis presented in this book, *gender* will be used in this sense of active negotiation. *Status*, following Linton's distinction between a particular position and the status of an individual, will be used in two ways. When in reference to a person, I have used status synonymously with prestige. When used in the abstract (as in *civilized status*) the term denotes a specific position in a hierarchy, but it should be kept in mind that such positions occur at the convergence of numerous other statuses. As will be demonstrated in Chapter 2, age, gender, and access to supernatural power are all statuses that converge at the upper levels of the traditional Glebo political structure. Likewise, civilization must be seen as a way of life acquired by those holding a series of other positions.

The problem that informs this case study, therefore, concerns the intersection of multiple systems of ranking in the persons of the civilized Glebo women of Cape Palmas. How do prestige categories constrain the lives of these women, and how are they actively manipulated, negotiated, and managed in the course of everyday life? How may common sociological concepts like status and class be rendered gender-sensitive so we can observe the different implications for a man or a woman occupying a particular position?

I will analyze the operation of gender and other status considerations in the lives of both civilized and native Glebo women, focusing on three specific areas: the organization of domestic units, the economic strategies available to women, and the social and cultural contributions of women to the Glebo community as a whole. The argument begins with a consideration of the categories of personhood salient for the Glebo, including locally and nationally defined positions of prestige. Chapter 3 provides a regional historical perspective and discusses the origins and development of the concept of civilization, culminating in an interpretation of the meaning of civilized status for the Glebo of today.

Chapters 4, 5, and 6 present the core of my research in Cape Palmas, building the case for the analysis of how women and men both uphold and challenge status categories through daily practice. Demographic data derived from a census of six communities provide structural evidence of the interdependent relationship between civilized and native households. This articulation is seen particularly in the area of child fosterage and the recruitment of new members to the civilized community. The economic relations that provide the material grounding of status competition and management are presented next, based on evidence from the census, participant observation with both civilized women and native female farmers, and a set of structured interviews with professional market women. Finally, the social and economic relations between women in different status categories are examined in the context of the ritual life of the Glebo community. Specifically, elaborate funerals appear to be important events at which civilized and native women must collaborate to discharge their obligations to the dead. It is in this context that the roles of civilized and native women are most clearly seen as complementary to each other rather than to the respective roles of civilized and native men.

The concluding chapter presents the results of this analysis as a framework for understanding the differential effects of status distinctions on women and men. Although the present work is limited to a small and obscure West African people, I believe the implications to be broader in scope. Feminist anthropology is only beginning to question and redefine taken-for-granted analytical constructs like class and status. This analysis of the Glebo is intended as a small contribution to the larger project.

[2]

Cape Palmas and the Glebo: Categories of Personhood

The Glebo locate persons in various ways in time and space; language, kinship, and relative age ground each individual in a series of social and political units. The ways in which gender and other forms of prestige and power intersect in Glebo culture give insights into social interactions. The identity of each individual, as rooted in a particular dialect group, "tribe," town, and patriclan, constitutes the basic Glebo "person," around which other ascribed and achieved statuses coalesce.

Linguistic and Political Categories of Personhood

Although southeastern Liberia has received considerable attention from professional historians (Brooks 1962, 1972; Davis 1968; Martin 1968; Sullivan 1978), there has been relatively little anthropological work in this area since George Schwab's expedition through the "Liberian hinterland" in the 1930s (1947). As Frederick D. McEvoy (whose 1971 dissertation on the Sabo is a welcome exception to the general neglect) notes, there has been serious controversy over the ethnic and linguistic classification of this area. Joseph H. Greenberg places the languages of the southeast within the Kwa (on Figure 1, "Kruan") subfamily of the Niger-Congo family (1963:8). The Liberian languages Kru, Grebo, Bassa, Krahn, and De (Dey) form a "Kru Group" within the subfamily (Figure 2). Southeasterners are therefore linguistically distinguished from

[15]

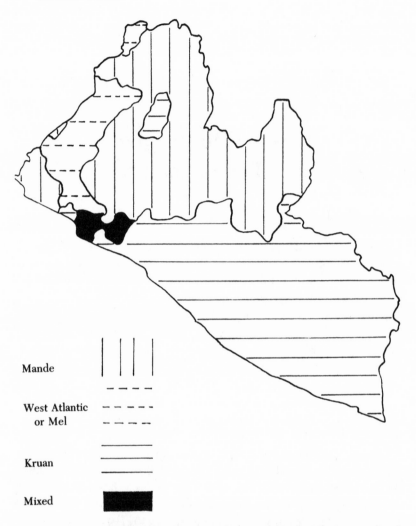

Figure 1. Liberian linguistic families (from Duitsman 1982–83:30). Reprinted with permission from *Liberian Studies Journal.*

northern and western Liberians, who speak languages of the West Atlantic and Mande subfamilies. The Kwa and West Atlantic speakers are assumed to be the oldest inhabitants of the Liberian rain forest; the Mande speakers are believed to have arrived more recently from the "nuclear Mande" area to the north (d'Azevedo 1962:517, 520–21, 524–25).

[16]

Figure 2. Liberian languages (from Duitsman 1982–83:31). Reprinted with permission from *Liberian Studies Journal.*

Within each of the larger language groups, Kru, Krahn, and Grebo, are numerous dialects with varying degrees of intelligibility. The Grebo-speakers of the Cape Palmas region claim to be able to "hear" but not "speak" most of the interior dialects, and some said they could "hear" Kru. I, with a limited knowledge of the "seaside" Grebo dialect, could sometimes "hear" friends in Monrovia who spoke one of the Krahn dialects. This mutual intelligibility over wide distances has contributed to the tendency to treat categories such as Kru and Grebo as if they described homogeneous ethnic groups or tribes (see McEvoy 1977). Southeasterners treat dialectical variation within languages as significant markers of social

[17]

and political difference, rather than as an indicator of common origin or shared interest. Dialects shift over very short distances; within fifteen miles from the coast, a significant difference in speech can be identified. Sometimes, but not always, dialect boundaries conform to recognized tribal (*dako*) boundaries. As McEvoy has noted, the *dako*, a patrilineally ascribed, territorially defined "citizenship," appears to be the most inclusive political identity with which southeastern Liberian peoples identify (ibid.:70). Some *dakwe* (plural form) consist only of a few villages, which trace their descent from a common ancestor and contain families belonging to the same named patrilineal clans (Figure 3).

The Cape Palmas people with whom I worked are usually considered as one *dako*, called Glebo or Gedebo, which is internally divided into two sections (ibid.:64; Martin 1968:10). The people themselves, however, while recognizing a common history and dialect, consider their sections to represent two distinct *dakwe*, the Nyomowe and the Kuniwe "tribes." Some informants even insist that the Nyomowe and Kuniwe speak different dialects, but the distinction is made on the basis of small differences in pronunciation. It is typical of the southeastern peoples in general, however, that political distinctions are phrased in terms of linguistic differences. At the minimal level, although I visited and worked with members of both coastal *dakwe* and some interior ones, my primary data come from the Nyomowe people of Cape Palmas, specifically, the towns of Gbenelu, Wuduke, Jeploke, Puduke, Waa Hodo Wodo, and the civilized town of Hoffman Station. Altogether, these six towns contain approximately three thousand people.

The Glebo-speaking *dakwe* inhabit a series of villages strung out on either side of Cape Palmas, covering a total distance of about thirty miles from Fishtown Point to the western bank of the Cavalla River (Johnston 1906:922; Martin 1968:2). Their own oral histories place them in this area no earlier than 1700, although European travelers reported trading with coastal peoples in this area since at least 1462 (Johnston 1906:43–44). The Glebo origin myth describes the wanderings of the original six (Johnson 1957:3) or eight (Wallace 1980:27–28) patrilineal clans (*pane*) from the interior of what is now Grand Gedeh County to the coast at Bereby in the present Ivory Coast. Migrating west along the coast, they founded two settle-

[18]

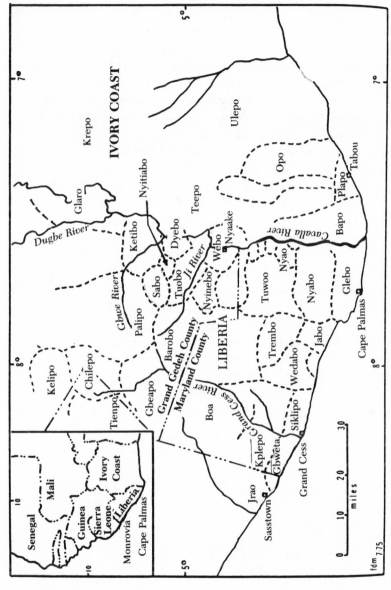

Figure 3. Grebo-speaking *dakwe* of the Cape Palmas region (from McEvoy 1977:63). Reprinted with permission from *Africa*, journal of the International African Institute.

ments, at Cape Palmas and at Rocktown Point, both located on strategic promontories above the sea. The Cape Palmas town was named Gbenelu, or "Assembly" because members of all the clans assembled there, and the Rocktown settlement, Taake, "place of medicine," because of its ritual importance. From these two towns originated the other Glebo towns along the coast; those settled by families from Gbenelu became Nyomowe and those from Taake were Kuniwe (Table 1). The distinction is sometimes expressed in terms of freshwater and saltwater; the Kuniwe reportedly took their name from a freshwater lake near Taake, and the Nyomowe took theirs from the Nyomo (now Hoffman) River, which is saline at its mouth (Johnson, 1957:19).

With one exception, Kuniwe territory encompasses the coast from Fishtown Point (Waa) up to but not including the town of Puduke on the west bank of the Nyomo. The Nyomowe area includes Cape Palmas itself and all coastline to the western bank of the Cavalla. The exception to this neat geographical division is a very powerful constellation of towns known as Gbede at the southernmost bend of the coast close to the Cavalla River. Colonized by disgruntled residents from Taake, it was and is a Kuniwe outpost in the center of Nyomowe territory. Hence many of the incessant wars between the two *dakwe* centered on this area (Martin 1968:44). Both groups also claim large tracts of "bush" land in the interior for making farms. Claims extend to tracts that had been farmed in the past and were abandoned to the seven- to twelve-year fallowing cycle, as well as untouched gallery forest to be cut for future farms.

Table 1. Glebo towns by *dako* affiliation

Nyomowe	Kuniwe
Gbenelu (Big Town)	Taake (Rocktown)
Wuduke	
Jeploke	
Puduke	
Blegye (Whole Graway)	Waa (Fishtown)
Glebogbade (Half Graway)	Seede (Middletown)
Yaake (King's Town)	Gbede (Grand Cavalla)
Wodeke	
Kablake (River Cavalla)	

The people of Gbenelu found themselves in an endless series of disputes with the residents of the Kuniwe town of Waa, whose farmlands were immediately adjacent to their own. The Kuniwe of Gbede were in a similarly antagonistic relationship with the Nyomowe towns of Blegye and Kablake. Enmity between these towns was still running high during 1982–83, and a court case over land was pending between Waa and Gbenelu.

Terms like *Grebo* and *Kru* have been adopted as ethnic labels by the Liberian government and are used in the census and other official publications. In recent years, it has been assumed that these categories follow the arbitrary boundaries between administrative units such as counties and districts; thus, in the official view, all the residents of Maryland County are Grebo, those of Sinoe County are Kru, and Grand Gedeh County is inhabited by a solid block of Krahn. The use of these labels has led to the belief that there are separate, distinct, and unified "tribes" called Grebo and Kru: exactly the "conventional misunderstandings" which McEvoy deplores (1977:62–64). For the purposes of this book, I will follow Martin's usage in reserving the term *Glebo* to refer to the thirteen Nyomowe and Kuniwe towns from Waa to Kablake. *Grebo* will be used to refer to other peoples of numerous *dakwe* (such as Nyabo, Jabo, and Sabo) who speak Grebo languages. Speakers of the many Kru languages will be referred to collectively as Kru, but it should be kept in mind that this usage does *not* indicate a common ethnic identity, except insofar as people have adopted these labels vis-à-vis the Liberian government.

Physically and geographically, the Glebo world is bounded by the contrast between rain forest and beach, farm village and coastal town, burned field and open sea. Although the towns are important social and political units, they are fully occupied only three months of the year. As shifting horticulturists of upland dry rice, the Glebo spend most of their time in the farm villages (usually only one or two houses, occupied by a single household) scattered throughout the interior rain forest and sometimes as far as a day's walk from the coast.

At the most basic level, there are really only two places a Glebo individual can be: at home in "we country" (*a bli*) or "gone stranger" (*mu daba*). Although both McEvoy (1971) and Jo Mary Sullivan

(1978) have emphasized *dako* identity in their discussion of interior Grebo and Kru peoples, the Glebo conception of "country" seems to center more on the territory claimed by a single town. A person's identity is tightly bound to where he or she is from, indicated by a town (rather than *dako*) affiliation, which, like *dako* and *pano*, or clan membership, is patrilineally acquired. Ideally, one is from the *dako*, town, and clan of one's father, independent of actual place of birth or residence; innumerable Glebo who were born abroad to parents working in Ghana or Nigeria "came home" as adults to ancestral towns which they had never seen. Likewise, a Glebo student in the United States explained to me that he is from Cape Palmas although he was born and raised in Monrovia, speaks no Glebo, and has visited Maryland County only once.

Although the Liberian government recognizes two chiefdoms among the Glebo and appoints paramount chiefs for both Nyomowe and Kuniwe, the Glebo *dakwe* do not act as internally coordinated political units. Each town tends to settle its own affairs, alone or with allies of its own choosing from within the *dako* or from other Grebo-speaking *dakwe*. There is even evidence to suggest that the *dako* identity of a town is flexible in response to shifting patterns of intermarriage or wartime political alliances. McEvoy reports that several towns belonging to the interior Sabo *dako* were considered to be not Sabo at all but "more Palibo" or "more Tuobo" because of strong matrilateral linkages with these other *dakwe* (1977:74). I would argue, then, that town identification is more salient for an individual's sense of self among the Glebo than is *dako* affiliation.

Kinship and Marriage in the Definition of Persons

The towns themselves are divided into quarters, each of which belongs to a different *pano*, or named patrilineal clan. The local branch of these trans-*dako* clans is likewise known as a *pano* or *kwa*. McEvoy uses the term *local sib element* to refer to similar groups among the Sabo (1971:198). Ideally, all local members of a given *pano* should reside within the same quarter of the town; in actuality, most have a number of resident strangers, and members of the clan may be residing in other areas for various reasons. Never-

[22]

theless, a specific *pano* in a specific town represents the exact point in space to which each Glebo individual "belongs."

Although all Glebo persons are grounded and defined in this way, the mechanism by which such an identity is ascribed is patrifiliation. This concept obviously means different things for men and women, especially since residence is patrilocal and a woman must leave her natal *pano,* and often her town and *dako* as well, at marriage. But *pane* (plural of *pano*) are not restricted to any particular town. According to the origin myth, representatives of the original six or eight families are believed to have joined in the settlement of each of the Glebo towns. If all *pane* were indeed once represented in each Glebo town, some have since become extinct and others have developed junior lines, which seem to be in the process of becoming *pane* in their own right. One small Nyomowe town, Yaake, currently has only two resident *pane,* while the powerful Blegye, a short walk along the beach to the south, has at least twelve. But a member of the *taagyudebo pano* from Yaake is "at home" in the *taagyudebo pano* of any town, even one belonging to another *dako.* Thus a Nyomowe must be welcomed by his or her "family" in a Kuniwe town, even at times of great inter-*dako* hostility between Nyomowe and Kuniwe. *Pano* ties even transcend dialect and language boundaries, as the Glebo claim to share *pano* designations with some interior Grebo- and Krahn-speaking groups as well as with the Kru-speaking coastal Siklipo *dako* to their west. The Glebo insist that they have the right to "just walk in the house and eat the food off the table" in any Kru *pano* that has the same name as their own and that, likewise, a Kru stranger has similar rights in their own homes, "because we are all one family." McEvoy refers to a similar relationship between the Sabo and certain Kru Coast *dakwe* (1971:194).

These *pano* relationships indicate that in-marrying women are likely to find a source of support in the local section of their *pano* in most southeastern towns. Although a woman may represent her marital *pano* on the women's council of elders and will ultimately be buried by her husband's clan, she never loses her own *pano* membership. "A woman does not perish in marriage" (Herzog and Blooah 1936:179) is a proverb collected from the neighboring Jabo which recognizes the lifelong connection between a married wom-

[23]

an and her family of origin. Although the payment of bridewealth ideally binds a woman to her husband and his clan for life or until full repayment, in practice marital status is often ambiguous and open to negotiation. Divorce is fairly easily obtained and may be initiated by either spouse. If the man sends his wife back to her natal *pano* without cause, however, he forfeits the bridewealth he gave for her. Men who desire a divorce usually mistreat or ignore their wives until the women leave of their own accord. A woman who wishes to marry another man will arrange to have her lover refund the bridewealth directly to her husband (Innes 1966:139).

Rights to a woman's reproductive potential as well as to her labor and sexual services are transferred with the payment of bride-wealth, usually one cow or its cash equivalent (about forty dollars in 1983), to the *pano* of the husband. On the death of her husband, a widow is required to choose a new partner from among the eligible males of the *pano*. She may return to her own *pano* if the bride-wealth is refunded by her family. The verb *to marry* (*pable*) in Glebo cannot be applied to a female subject; informants found it impossible to construct the phrase "She married him" in either Glebo or English. A man marries a woman, who is then said to be "married to" his *pano* or even to his town, as in the common phrase "she married to Blegye," expressing the reality of patrilocal resi-dence.

Some form of marriage is expected of all normally functioning individuals. Both men and women are assumed to have strong sexual needs and desires, which may be harmful if not given a proper outlet. Pubescent women are seen as especially sexually rapacious and difficult to control; this explanation often justifies early betrothal and marriage among native Glebo. A certain amount of sexual experimentation is expected of young people of both sexes, and there is little formal concern with virginity. But the flirtations of young women are viewed as a major cause of conflict among men and resentment among already married women. Moth-ers attempt to keep their daughters too occupied with work in the house or on the farm to spend much time "strolling" around town.

Innes's grammatical description of the Glebo language (1966) contains a remarkable text contributed by a Glebo informant in

London. The first paragraph conveys the full flavor of Glebo eroticism and notions of romantic love:

> It is well known that a man and woman do not rush into marriage. They must know each other first as lovers. However, lovemaking does not wait for maturity and old age, hence children make love, just as adults do. When you see young love, you think it is more pleasant than adult love. When you are children, love begins on the beach. At play, you smear your companion with mud, your companion hits you with a lump of earth. This goes on for some time before you come to know each other well. The two of you who are choosing each other imitate married life there on the beach. When the time for playing hide and seek arrives, it is you two who hide by yourselves. If you see a nut and break it, you eat part and put part aside for your companion. At home, when your mother gives you food, you work a handful of rice into a lump and look for your companion to give it to. If you come into a crowd, nobody touches your companion without your coming to blows over it. Nothing comes near this for sweetness and pleasantness. This is what we have in mind when we say, 'Kpoa says, "A child's play is pleasant."' (ibid.:132)

The text continues with a description of courtship, bridewealth negotiations, the process of becoming married, tips for managing a harmonious polygynous household, and the eventual decline and demise of some unions. In tone, it conveys the romantic, unfearful, playful manner in which the Glebo approach matters of sex and reproduction. I found no evidence of any menstrual restrictions on women, although ideas of hygiene dictate that a woman should have a special basket in which to keep her menstrual cloths and that she should wash them separately from the clothing of the family. Getting wet in the rain and crossing bodies of water are felt to be potentially harmful to the health of menstruating women, but these beliefs do not seem to restrict their mobility. In former times, a two-year postpartum taboo on sexual intercourse was enforced to protect the nursing child from milk "spoiled" by male semen; Glebo men often cited this custom in justifying polygyny to disapproving missionaries. The practice of a postpartum taboo appears to have declined in recent years, although some women still say it is "good to rest" for a year or two after the birth of a child.

[25]

Age Categories and Personhood

Kinship and local identities endure for life, but other categories of personhood are tied to individual life cycles. As each Glebo town is divided spatially into *pane*, it is divided temporally by the succession of age cohorts among its residents. The passage of time is often measured by the lifetime of an individual; larger regional or national events tend to be dated in terms of the lives of past Liberian presidents. Exact genealogical memory is shallow; births and deaths within a particular family are often reckoned according to the life cycle of a particular elder, as in "it happened when Kla was a young man, going to Ghana for the first time." Relative chronological age is an important ranking mechanism, particularly for men.

The Glebo recognize well-defined age groups for men and less categorical grades for women. Early sources such as John Payne (1845) and J. L. Wilson (1856) contain detailed descriptions which differ little from later accounts (Wallace 1955; Johnson 1957) and from the present situation. The following divisions are recognized among a town's resident males: the *kyinibo*, also called the *pede nyinibo* (my own attempt at translation renders this term as "those who neglect to look after their own excrement"), or "small boys" from about four to twelve years old. With girls of similar age, they constitute the *wodo yudu*, town children, but unlike girls they have great freedom to play and are required to make little economic contribution. They are sometimes used as messengers by town elders or recruited to keep the town's paths and open spaces free of brush (Johnson 1957:53). The *kinibo*, young unmarried men, in earlier times were frequently away from home on migrant labor trips. They were occasionally used as an internal police force to carry out the judgments of the town as a whole. The *sidibo* or *gbo* were the soldiers or warriors in former times; today, as then, they include all adult married men who belong patrilineally to the town. McEvoy reports that the Sabo *gbo* are internally stratified by age into four subgrades (1971:181), but I have seen no evidence of similar organization among the Glebo. Jane Jackson Martin has suggested that precolonial Glebo intratown politics consisted of a protracted power struggle between the *sidibo* and the *gbudubo*, or elders (1968:19–20). Also known as *nyekbade* or, after the religious structure in which they meet, *takae,* the elders were undoubtedly the most powerful group in precolonial Glebo society. Another name for them was *jiwodo,* leopard's mouth, for their ability to impose fines (Johnson 1957:54), and this power is greatly feared even today. Technically, no adult Glebo man or woman is supposed to leave town for any extended period without informing and receiving the permission of the *gbudubo.* Failure to do so might result in the order to bring a cow on the traveler's return.

Glebo women appear to be less stratified by age than men, and a set of named female groups similar to that of the men's does not exist. McEvoy argues that this is because a significant portion of the adult females in any town have married in from other towns and *dakwe,* thereby making it difficult to know their exact ages. McEvoy's male Sabo informants asserted that women lacked elaborate age classifications because "women are women—they do not need those things" (1971:171–72). I received similar responses from Glebo men: "Mostly, we just call them 'women.'" Although Payne described the Glebo women of Gbede as being "divided into two or three classes according to their ages, who dance together and have certain regulations and privileges as a community" (1845:115), other references are scanty and questionable, particularly in the face of denial by Glebo women themselves that they are organized into groups directly analogous to those of the men.

The Cultural Construction of Gender, Power, and Prestige

There are three primary sources of power and prestige in native Glebo society: gender, relative age, and position in the formal political structure. These are not the only sources of power which the Glebo recognize; some economic stratification has been present since the fifteenth century, when Glebo men first became involved in the coastal trade with Europeans. These three sources seem to be indigenous to the culture, however, and they remain most available to people who consider themselves natives. These areas of power and prestige are not distinct but intersect and interpenetrate in numerous ways. They are also gender-sensitive, meaning that all

[27]

three are equally available to men and to women, but with different manifestations and consequences.

The Glebo believe that all human beings have the capacity for purposeful work. Work includes cooking, cleaning, and all tasks connected with household maintenance and agricultural production as well as sexual intercourse ("it takes a lot of work to make a human being"), childbirth, ritual dancing, the holding of political offices, and the execution of duties related to those offices. The practice of *we*, witchcraft, and other ritual activities such as sacrifices, the consulting of oracles, and divination are also considered work.

Most practical tasks are divided into men's and women's work. As is typical of this area of West Africa, which has been dubbed "the female farming belt" (Boserup 1970; Lancaster 1976), women are primarily responsible for raising subsistence crops, particularly rice and cassava, as well as additional staples such as pepper, eggplant, okra, and greens. Men help clear the fields at the beginning of the agricultural cycle in late January, felling and burning the trees and constructing fences around the perimeter of the field to keep out rodents and other pests. Women sow, weed, harvest, and process the crop and recruit children to assist with these tasks and with "bird-scaring" while the vulnerable rice is ripening. During this period, men may be involved in hunting, fishing, cultivating cash crops like rubber or sugarcane, or gathering forest products such as palm nuts and palm wine for consumption or sale. Some men reside in the coastal towns during most of the year while their wives are on the farms in the interior; others are away much of the time pursuing wage labor on rubber plantations or in iron mines.

This sexual division of labor is reflected in the cultural ideal of the hardworking wife, the provider for her household. Husbands are expected to supply their wives with gifts, but any income men receive from cash crops or wage labor is not automatically considered part of the household budget. Likewise, women have exclusive control over market profits from the sale of surplus agricultural produce. A married couple, therefore (and men and women in general), is not seen as engaged in complementary tasks leading to a common goal. Rather, each is engaged in separate lines of productive work while sharing a joint interest in the welfare of the domestic unit to which they both belong.

[28]

The Glebo cultural construction of gender, therefore, does not characterize women as the complementary opposites of men. Instead, men and women seem to constitute different types of human beings (see Rogers 1978 on the implications of this gender ideology). As an example, Glebo men are often described as warriors, but women are not relegated to the position of nonwarriors. Glebo women are also referred to as warriors in a number of contexts, particularly those involving suffering and danger, such as childbirth. The dances that are performed to honor the death of an adult, the *doklo,* which is danced by men for a deceased man, and the *nana,* danced by women for a woman, are both referred to as "war dances." The point here is that powerful or high-status categories such as warrior, witch, or chief are not restricted to one gender over the other. But, a woman warrior (or chief, or witch) is inherently different from a man warrior.

All status positions in Glebo society may therefore be viewed as gender-sensitive, as having significantly different characteristics depending on whether they are filled by men or women. Clearly, both men and women have access to the status that accompanies growing old in Glebo society. A surprising (for a largely nonliterate society) number of people know the exact year of their birth, and many households keep a small notebook recording the birth dates of all family members. But even when it can be strictly determined, one's age among the Glebo is relative to that of the oldest living members of the community. Since a certain percentage of the population is always elderly, no Glebo is considered fully grown until over the age of fifty, at the very least. I have heard men and women in their forties referred to and refer to themselves as "small boys" and "small girls." This usage contrasts with that of big and small elsewhere in West Africa, where these terms refer to wealth and power rather than chronological age (Sanjek, personal communication). Though big and small sometimes have this same connotation in Liberia, a number of impoverished elderly people among the Glebo were known as undeniably big because of their advanced age and demonstrated wisdom. To become old is to succeed to the previous generation as it passes on; one prominent civilized man in his fifties explained that he still belonged to the *gofa,* or youth, because some of his teachers were still living and, since they were

[29]

undeniably old, he could not consider himself their equal. It is therefore not possible to determine the exact age at which someone becomes an elder, or even an adult. Because of the different cycles of birth and death within each family, the status of each individual must be considered on its own basis.

Relative age is used as a metaphor to describe the hierarchical relationship between the genders. "Men are always older than women" is a common expression of the Glebo ideal of patriarchy. Although this saying is not acted upon literally (for instance, young sons do not attempt to assert status over their mothers), it is a clear example of the collapsing of one status hierarchy into another. Men are entitled to dominance over women by virtue of their gender, just as older men are entitled to dominance over younger men by virtue of their age. The difference, of course, is that young men will someday become old men, but a woman will never "outgrow" any man; gender overrides other status markers in this case. In their separate political institutions, women may direct their own affairs, but relative to men their status is lower.

As it intersects with gender, age is likewise incorporated into the official political organization of Glebo towns. Here, once again, the important consideration is of age relative to that of others. Unlike the other male age grades, a man does not succeed automatically to the *gbudubo,* or council of elders, on the basis of age alone; rather, it is a question of his age relative to the other males of his *pano.* Only the oldest man in each local branch of the clan represents his *pano* on the town's *gbudubo.* As a result, some very elderly men remain *sidibo* (soldiers) for their entire lives because of the longevity of a slightly older relative.

Each *pano* also has a female representative to the *gbudubo,* who is likewise the oldest woman resident in the quarter, either an in-marrying member of another *pano* or a natal daughter of the clan. At the level of townwide political offices, the separation of male and female hierarchies among the Glebo conforms to Kamene Okonjo's description of "dual-sex political organization" in which "each sex manages its own affairs and women's interests are represented at all levels" (1976:45). As I have argued elsewhere (Moran 1989), the important point here is that women are represented politically by other women. Thus the delegates to the women's council of elders represent not their respective *pane* but the women of those clans, whether natal citizens of the town or in-marrying wives from other towns and *dakwe.* This distinction, I believe, is why a *pano* can send as its female representative a member of another *pano.*

The cultural construction of the genders as distinctly different types of persons is manifestated politically in the existence of separate male and female councils. Meeting together, the two groups form the *takae,* a name taken from that of the central ritual structure where this body meets. In Gbenelu in 1982–83, the word *takae* to refer to both male and female councils was more common than *gbudubo,* although this term is also used. Male elders tended to be referred to as the *takae,* while the parallel women's group was known as the women's *takae.* This qualification may be taken as a reminder that dual-sex political organization does not imply political parity. Yet the Glebo women do control their own political organizations and wield real power over both men and women through their ability, like the men's council, to impose fines. I have seen the women's *takae* of Gbenelu collect a five-dollar fine from the Nyomowe paramount chief for allegedly preventing one of his wives from attending a women's dance; he protested that she herself had chosen not to come, but he paid the fine.

Historically, political offices among the Glebo carried more prestige than real power over the lives of others. Although the different Glebo lineages are not hierarchically ranked (as are those of the Kpelle, see Bledsoe 1980), certain town positions are said to belong to particular *pane* (see Johnson 1957:42–57; see also McEvoy 1971 for comparable data on the Sabo). These include the positions of *wodo baa* (usually glossed as town father but actually translating to something more on the order of the town's namesake) and *bodio,* or high priest, both male offices. The corresponding female offices, the *blo nyene* (literally ground woman or women's president) and *gyide,* the high priest's wife, are not allocated by *pano* membership but are acquired through election and marriage, respectively.

The *wodo baa* of today has become fused with the Liberian government position of town chief. Even with this added legitimacy, the *wodo baa* remains a largely ceremonial office with no legislative or executive power. He presides over the *tapanu,* or assembly of all the town's residents, primarily as a moderator. By definition, the *wodo baa* is a member of the council of elders and

[31]

represents his *pano* in that body. He is among the first to be served kola, food, or drink at any ceremonial occasion but must also distribute these symbols of hospitality with a liberal hand to the many visitors who come to his house. He may hear cases in his "court," usually marital disputes, cases of petty theft, and so on, but has little authority to enforce his judgments. Since most of the Glebo centers consist of clusters of towns (e.g., the Gbenelu constellation includes the towns of Wuduke, Jeploke, Waa Hodo Wodo, Puduke, and the mission town of Hoffman Station), the *wodo baabo* (plural of *wodo baa*) often sit as a sort of chiefly council in hearing cases and at all ceremonial events.

Unlike the proliferation of *wodo baabo,* each cluster of Glebo towns has only one high priest, or *bodio.* As Martin has noted, the *bodio* shares some of the same features as the "divine kings" of many other African societies (1968:16). The *bodio* and his wife, the *gyide,* occupy the cult house, or *takae,* which contains the medicines regulating the health and success of the town and its citizens. The *takae* also serves as the meeting place of the *gbudubo* when there are important matters to be discussed. The structure itself is surrounded by a fence (usually a circle of posts stuck into the ground) past which no member of another *dako* is supposedly allowed. There are exceptions to this rule, however; I was invited inside the fence to photograph the *bodio* and his family at the *takae* of Gbenelu, and at least one stranger was allowed inside a Glebo *takae* and was permitted to handle the medicines (Martin, personal communication 1984).

The only requirement for the *gyide* is that she be from the same *dako* as her husband; since she has a part in keeping safe the medicines of the town, a stranger could not be trusted in times of inter-*dako* war or tension. A *bodio* may have other wives, but they have no ritual duties. Both *bodio* and *gyide* risk death, either supernaturally or at the hands of the town, if they commit adultery while in office, and an elaborate pattern of avoidance and respectful behavior limits their contact with unrelated people of the opposite sex (Johnson 1957:45–48). Although their economic support from the townspeople has declined in recent years, the *bodio* and *gyide* are still greatly respected and have great prestige. "You don't play with those people" is frequently heard.

[32]

Whereas the *gyide* acquires her position through marriage, and her ritual duties and privileges are similar to those of her husband, the *blo nyene* holds the independent position of leader of the town's women. McEvoy reports a similar office for Sabo, the *nyinokei*, which is also not hereditary and for which the major qualifications appear to be age and speaking ability. The *nyinokei* sits as the representative of the women on the men's council and "reports to and may argue with the male council the views of the village's women on any particular policy-making decision that involves the whole of the town's population" (1971:176). Like *blo nyene, nyinokei* is translated into English as the women's chief, the women's chairman, and even the women's president. Male and female Glebo informants told me that the *blo nyene* has ultimate veto power over any decision made by the men: "If she says no, then it is finished." Women add that the men "must listen to her." When she appears at public events accompanied by the town women or female clan elders, her way is cleared by young men, who serve as her "messengers" ringing large brass handbells (see McEvoy 1971:179 for similarities with the Sabo). The bells are also used to call all the women of the town together for meetings or dances. The *blo nyene* is often referred to as "our mother," and her title carries a clear association with the earth, or ground, but also with country or nation in a political sense (Innes 1967:12). If, as is claimed, the *blo nyene* actually has veto power over council decisions, then her authority extends much further than that of the *wodo baa*, or town chief.

Other native offices include two men's positions associated with the *sidibo* age grade, the *yibadio* and the *tibawa*. Both wear black clothing similar to that of the *bodio* and both offices are "owned" by particular *pane*. In earlier times, the *yibadio* and *tibawa* had important functions as generals or war priests; one was responsible for leading the troops into battle while the other brought up the rear and organized retreats, if necessary. Today, these offices are primarily ceremonial, and their only duties revolve around the *doklo*, or men's war dance, performed as part of funeral services. As "speakers" for the *sidibo*, however, these two positions have or have had important political implications. The speakers play a central role in managing the ongoing competition for decision-making

[33]

power between the elders and the younger men. When the military organization of a town was vital to its survival, these officers were probably considerably more influential.

Among Glebo women, the dance-leading functions of the *yibadio* and the *tibawa* are analogous to the role played by the *maasan,* or woman's dance coordinator. There are usually several women holding this position in a Glebo town, but there may be only a single *maasan,* and only one is needed during the dance itself. The *maasan,* like the *blo nyene,* is elected by all the women on the basis of her skill at dancing, and one of her responsibilities is teaching the complex series of steps to the young girls. Equipped with a police whistle, which is at once the symbol of her office and the means of crowd control, the *maasan* dances alone in front of the drums, coordinating changes in tempo with the male drummers and deciding the steps to be performed. Glebo women, like the men, dance in a long line that snakes single file around the town, sometimes doubling back on itself. The *maasan* must keep order in the line and keep it moving so that only a short section is actually performing in front of the drummers (and the spectators) at any one time. She must also shoo children away from the dance area and push back the press of the audience, all the while blowing furiously on her whistle in time with the beat and displaying the right way to dance. The *maasan* accompanies the *blo nyene* when she travels with the *gbudubo* on visits to other towns or makes a grand entrance to a public event in her own town. Male officials such as the *wodo baa, yibadio,* and *tibawa* are heralded by trumpeters with wooden "war horns" and by the clanging iron rattles carried by the *sidibo.* Although she has no acknowledged political function, the *maasan* is considered a "big woman" in the town, and her skill as an artist is admired and prized.

Local Administration and the Liberian State

Over this indigenous structure of diffused power and crosscutting rights and duties, the Liberian government in the early twentieth century superimposed its own system of indirect rule (Akpan 1973). A hierarchy of paramount, clan, town, and quarter chiefs was devised for all indigenous Liberians, regardless of whether they in any way resembled the indigenous divisions of legitimate power. In the southeast, chiefdoms were established corresponding roughly with *dako* boundaries, each headed by a paramount chief. The present paramount chiefs are usually elected by the people and confirmed by either the county superintendent (an appointed government post analogous to a U.S. state governor) or by the district supervisor (also an appointment from the national level, with authority over an administrative division within a county). Paramount chiefs are almost invariably men from families that "own" the *wodo baa* position or are otherwise prominent in the town.

The position of clan chief seems to correspond to no known indigenous role in any of the Liberian ethnic groups; it is entirely a creation of the central government. A clan is supposed to be an administrative subdivision within the chiefdom, although in the southeast the position always seems to go to someone already holding the *wodo baa* title. Town chiefs are almost always taken from the ranks of those eligible to be *wodo baabo,* and the office of quarter chief, supposedly the administrative head of a section of a town, has apparently never been successfully imposed on the Glebo. Although they are said to be elected by all the people, the men who rise to these government positions are actually chosen by the *gbudubo,* or lineage elders, who continue to make most of the decisions thereafter, although, when dealing with the central government, such decisions are carried out in the name of the chief.

The paramount chief actually has little executive power. At worst, he may become intensely unpopular because he must carry out certain government functions such as collecting taxes and imposing fines. He usually has one or more messengers who serve as policemen, bringing in offenders to his court and managing his appointments. A politically sensitive chief will rely on the advice and consent of the *gbudubo* in most cases. Since he will likely become the object of envy and resentment, he will need their help not only to sway the populace but to fend off the witchcraft that will certainly be directed against him. McEvoy's work on the Sabo includes an interesting discussion of the negotiations between the chiefs, in their roles as officials of national government, and the town elders, a contrast which is especially clear since the Sabo do not seem to

[35]

merge the position of chief and *wodo baa* (1971:168–71). In both cases, decision-making and executive power seem to remain diffused among ritual, age-grade, and women's leaders rather than being localized in those offices recognized by the Liberian government.

Just as local Glebo political organization might be termed "dual-sex," in Okonjo's words, the national set of offices imposed by the government is based on the Western single-sex model. The system of administrative chiefs contains no separate and distinct political roles for women, nor does it recognize their form of organization as political. Although several women have held the position of paramount, clan, and town chief in northwestern Liberia, none have yet attained this status among southeastern peoples. I suspect that the failure of southeastern women to rise within the single-sex hierarchy is because both men and women have equated it with the exclusively male positions under the indigenous system. The Glebo tendency to merge the *wodo baa* with the status of government chief marks that position as inherently male, while the government's ignorance, or ignoring, of the existing status of the *blo nyene* ensures that she does not receive the legitimacy (or the salary) of a chief. The increasing concentration of cash, in the form of a government salary, and of the right to use legitimate force (the paramount chief can, in theory, call in the national police to back him up if he wishes) may have enhanced the male side of the dual-sex organization at the expense of the female side. More historical and ethnographic data would be necessary to substantiate or refute such a hypothesis, but the situation is reminiscent of other places in which single-sex hierarchies have been imposed over dual-sex forms, to the detriment of women's control over their own affairs (Okonjo 1976; Van Allen 1972, 1976; Ardener 1975; Moran 1989).

Occult Power

Age and sociopolitical standing are important measures of an individual's power and prestige, but there is another form of power which the Glebo recognize. This is the seemingly pan-African philosophy of causation and human action in the world, which carries the unfortunate English gloss of *witchcraft*. When I discussed this topic with my informants, they asked about witchcraft in my country. When I claimed that it did not exist in America, they were skeptical. Were there such things as trees and grass in my country? If so, then there must also be "witch." The Glebo word *we* (witchcraft, bad medicine, occult practices, Innes 1967:121) carries this notion of a natural power or energy inherent in all living things. Indeed, "witch" may be recognized as the force of life itself, existing in varying degrees in people, plants, animals, and unusual inanimate objects such as large rocks. In human beings, the power increases with the age of the individual and knowledge of its use. Witchcraft is also sometimes discussed as a commodity to be bought and sold, a set of ritual manipulations that can be taught. It can be employed for either good or evil, but in the hands of human beings it is used most often to kill. As a theory of causation, "witch" explains, for example, why three children in one household die while their neighbors do not, even though both households use the same well, which everyone agrees is polluted.

Since it is frequently likened to knowledge, witchcraft is assumed to be a function of age; anyone who becomes an elder is acknowledged to be a witch. As the argument goes, everyone who survives to old age must be a witch in order to have avoided death for so long. All three major sources of power, age, political position, and witchcraft, may therefore be seen to merge at the highest levels. All of the *gbudubo* are said to be witches, but their respected position within Glebo society keeps their power turned to the general good. In finding out and punishing those accused of witchcraft, however, they must have help from the country doctors, or *diobo* (singular, *dio*). The *diobo* are themselves powerful witches and gain their initial power through having killed and ritually "eaten" at least one victim in company with others of their "society." Once possessed of *we*, they turn their efforts to selling their services for a fee as specialists in telling fortunes, removing curses, providing love potions, prophecy, and divination. A *dio* is also called in whenever a town has experienced a rash of unexplained deaths to discover who is responsible or to examine a suspect.

In keeping with the recognition that everyone in a small, face-to-face community will have some grudge or grievance against almost

[37]

everyone else, *diobo* are usually called in from another *dako*, often from a great distance away. A *dio* must preside over the famous "sassywood" trial by ordeal, common throughout Liberia, in which the suspect drinks an infusion made from the poisonous bark of the sasswood tree and either vomits to prove his or her innocence or dies of its effects, combining the discovery of guilt and the infliction of punishment all at one time. Although trials by sasswood, or *gyudu*, have been technically outlawed by the Liberian government, the practice is widespread, even in Monrovia itself. During my stay in Cape Palmas, at least three people died of the ordeal while another vomited and survived.

Both men and women can attain the status of *dio*, and women are held to be somewhat more adept than men, often combining their magical practice with trade in herbal medicines and sometimes even with Christian faith healing. According to legend, a woman first found the power of *we*, witchcraft, where Nysoa, the creator-god, had carelessly left it; with this power, the woman brought death into the world for the first time. She herself died a victim of the first *gyudu* trial, but not before passing along the secret of *we* to her children. From that time on, the knowledge spread rapidly, and Nysoe, disgusted with the evil of human beings, retired to heaven, where he would not have to watch them killing each other. Women are said to turn to witchcraft for comparatively petty reasons such as a quarrel with a co-wife or the inattention of a husband. It is possible that these beliefs stem from the very real contradiction between women's economic autonomy and the cultural ideal of male dominance in the household.

What is truly sobering about the Glebo conception of the power of witchcraft is that it is not only available to specialists like the *diobo* or to the oldest and structurally more powerful members of the community. The all-pervasive power of *we* can be appropriated by all whose "heart is strong" enough to use it, including even very young children. Children and adolescents, in fact, are often likely suspects precisely because of their structurally inferior position. Numerous stories attest to the tension between the generations in Glebo society; for example, youngsters may become vexed with the amount of work required of them, for being punished by an elder, or because of what they perceive as harsh and stingy treatment.

[38]

Young people are rarely forced to the *gyudu* ordeal; rather, they will be accused, will confess publicly, and perhaps name others who have been instructing them.

The Glebo conception of the practice of witchcraft appears fairly instrumental; a medicine is usually said to have been buried in the ground somewhere in the vicinity of the intended victim, and the object of most investigations is to get the witch to confess and reveal the exact spot of the medicine so it may be rendered harmless. In other cases, leaves or grasses may be place in close association with the victim, such as under his or her bed or among clothing or introduced into the food as poison. Unlike the "evil eye" of Europe, witchcraft for the Glebo is never the unintentional result of envy or resentment; it requires the actual manipulation of objects. Because of the close personal contact required, members of the victim's household are always suspected when a death occurs. This suspicion also recognizes the structural conditions whereby one's own family, the very people to whom one owes and expects loyalty and protection, are precisely the people one is most likely to quarrel with or offend. A favorite proverb that expresses this contradiction is "If the house will not sell you, the street cannot buy you." In other words, it is unlikely that an outsider can cause an individual serious harm without the consent and even active aid of a household member.

Female relatives are often prime suspects in such cases because their role in cooking gives them ample opportunity for harm. Cooking and eating are central metaphors for power in the supernatural realm; "cooked" people are those chosen by the elders to be ritually treated in a way that will allow them to detect and identify witches in the community. One joins a witchcraft society by "eating witch" and continues symbolically to eat those who are killed with this power. The strong association of women with cooking and of cooking with witchcraft points up the belief that women are the most powerful and dangerous of witches. The use of these metaphors indicates the dark side of the usually joyous appreciation of good food in Glebo culture. Food is always a likely medium for the introduction of poison, making a woman's responsibility for watching over and protecting food crucial to the well-being of her household. Rice and soup that have been left unattended for a sus-

[39]

piciously long period of time are dumped out uneaten, and people express more concern about possible intruders tampering with the family's food than they do about theft.

We, then, is a form of free-flowing power which is available to all and is often the recourse of those people (women, young people) who occupy structurally inferior positions in the social hierarchy. That hierarchy itself, with its well-defined series of positions, is also a form of power and, even more, of prestige. The young woman who is accused of killing an older kinsman through witchcraft may be a figure to be feared, but she is not esteemed by the community in the same way as an elderly male chief, known to have killed many with his power, yet now, as a member of the *gbudubo*, concerned with protecting the community from just such antisocial acts.

In all these areas of status, prestige, and power, it is clear that gender is intertwined in significant ways with the attainment and form of an individual's standing in the Glebo community. It is therefore hardly surprising that new status distinctions, entering from other cultural traditions, should likewise be gender-sensitive.

[3]

Civilization: Historical Development and Present Meaning

Elizabeth Tonkin has claimed that "civilization . . . got to Liberia before the Liberians" (1981:310), and the significance of this statement is revealed in the history of European coastal trade with West Africa. The Glebo and other coastal peoples were long aware of a variety of lifestyles besides their own. This chapter describes the historical development of the civilized/native dichotomy in Glebo culture, its relationship to the economic structure of the country, and the way it has become embodied in Liberian law.

Historical Background: The Coastal Economy

Cape Palmas, or Cape of Palms, was named by Portuguese explorers for its most distinguishing feature. The cape is a strategic point on the West African coast, marking the boundary between the Windward and Leeward coasts. John H. B. Latrobe noted in the 1820s that, because of the direction of the prevailing winds, Cape Palmas was the last point from which a safe and easy return to the Cape Verde Islands could be made by a sailing vessel in any season (1885:94). This crucial climatological feature has contributed to the long and complex relationship between European visitors and all the coastal peoples of southeastern Liberia. Today, Cape Palmas is the southern and easternmost administrative center in the republic of Liberia and the official frontier with its neighbor to the east, the Ivory Coast.

[41]

Sir Harry Johnston (1906) reports that the recognizable outline of Cape Palmas appears on a Genoan map of Africa dated 1351, at least a century before it was mapped and named by the Portuguese. He suggests, however, that the map was based on information given by "Moors and Arabs" to Italian geographers. The first recorded exploration of the southern Liberian coast was by the Portuguese navigator Pedro de Sintra in 1462, probably extending as far as the mouth of the Cavalla. In the years following, the coast from Sherbro Island to the San Pedro River became known as the Grain Coast, a reference not to rice or wheat but to grains of pepper, the region's most valuable export commodity (Johnston 1906:35–36, 43–44).

Although they maintained a virtual monopoly on the West African trade for almost a century, the Portuguese were slowly succeeded by the Dutch, French, and English. Johnston notes, "At the beginning of the seventeenth century, travellers record that the natives along the Liberian coast were becoming tri-lingual; that is to say, in addition to their native language they could speak Portuguese and English." A list of European goods traded for pepper and ivory by a British captain at the mouth of the Sino River in 1555 includes basins, iron knives, bracelets, and beads, and the report of a sea battle between an English ship and a fleet of more than one hundred Kru canoes indicates that business was not always smooth (ibid.:49, 65, 67–68). For the most part, however, the Europeans seem to have been favorably impressed with the people they met, commenting on their strong physique and courtesy toward strangers.

The earliest reference specifically to the people of Cape Palmas comes from Pacheco Pereira, who called them Eguerebo around 1500 (Hair 1967:257). In (or about) 1614 the German geographer Levinus Hulsius referred to them as Gruvo, which Johnston suggests might have been corrupted to Grubo and hence to Kruboy, the name applied to all Grain Coast inhabitants who took employment on European ships (1906:85, n. 1). The geographer Olfert Dapper appears to have been the first to extend the label Kru or Krau to all the peoples of the southeast coast, a tendency that continues to produce confusion even today (see McEvoy 1977; Brooks 1972). Johnston reports that although it was acknowledged that the languages spoken on either side of the cape were similar, by the beginning of the eighteenth century mariners were distinguishing between "the fiercely cannibal tribes of what is now the Ivory Coast and the more sophisticated Krumen on the hither side of Cape Palmas" (1906:91–92). By the eighteenth century, the people of this area were reportedly taking European names and speaking a mixed trade jargon of Portuguese and English.

The "sophisticated Krumen" did not limit themselves only to trade with passing ships. From about the 1780s, temporary labor migration aboard European ships and in port cities from Freetown to Luanda became the norm for young men from this region (Brooks 1972; Davis 1968; Martin 1982). Although collectively known as Krumen, undoubtedly a large number of these were Glebo- and other Grebo-speakers, since Cape Palmas rapidly became an important center for labor recruitment, with about two thousand men shipped out yearly by 1873 (Martin 1982:1; 1968:52).

The Krumen who returned from these voyages and extended stays in foreign parts were worldly and experienced beyond those who had stayed behind, as well as wealthier. Much of this wealth, in the form of trade goods rather than cash, was handed over by the young travelers to their town elders and moved quickly into distribution networks as bridewealth, repayment of debts, and gifts (Brooks 1972:2). Besides acquiring a facility with European languages, migrants occasionally had the opportunity to acquire more formal education, and some came back literate in both foreign languages and their own (Wallace 1983). Southeastern coastal peoples quickly developed a taste for items of European manufacture. Traditional formal male dress for the Glebo, at the time of American colonization and today, consists of a long-sleeved white shirt, dark suit coat, tie, and bowler hat worn over a wraparound cloth or *lappa* that reaches to the floor. Tonkin perceptively notes that many of the attributes of the concept of civilization preceded both American settlers and Christian missionaries to Liberia.

Significantly, it was exclusively male labor which was recruited by the Europeans. Shipboard life made bringing wives and children impractical, and the "Krutowns" that sprang up in cities like Freetown, Monrovia, and Accra were for the most part male-only compounds until the late nineteenth century (Fraenkel 1964; Brooks 1972; Davis 1968). The preference for hiring men was a result of the intersection of European and African ideas about the sexual division of labor. Europeans would have been unlikely to consider hiring women as deck hands and the "Kru" women were occupied almost year-round with agricultural work (see Moran 1986). Indeed, according to all the European accounts, the stated purpose for which the Krumen hired themselves out was to acquire enough cash and goods to "purchase" a wife, who would then stay home and "make farm" while he went on another trip to earn money for his next marriage. The tradition of migrant labor as a significant event in young manhood and a major step toward maturity and standing in the community was widespread throughout southeastern Liberia, even far to the interior among such groups as the Sabo (McEvoy, 1971). Men, therefore, have always had a privileged access to employment, education, and the constellation of material and attitudinal traits that later came to be called "civilized." Their head start was reinforced and perpetuated with the arrival of the Maryland settlers and the Episcopal missionaries who accompanied them.

Colonial History: Maryland in Liberia

Liberia, the oldest black republic in Africa, has an unusual history. It was founded by a private benevolent organization as a solution to the problem of "free people of color" in the antebellum United States. As early as the American Revolution, thinkers such as Thomas Jefferson foresaw the end of chattel slavery in the New World. But late eighteenth- and early nineteenth-century writers found it impossible to visualize a multiracial society in which former slaves could be absorbed as free citizens. When Sierra Leone was founded as a colony for British former slaves in 1787, repatriation to Africa became an attractive possibility (Staudenraus 1961:2, 8). Although Liberia was never an official colony of the United States, the first settlement at Monrovia in 1822 received military protection from the U.S. Navy and supplies and colonial administrators from its sponsor, the American Colonization Society (ACS). By 1847, the string of settlements perched tenuously along the coast declared independence as the republic of Liberia (for a full discussion of the colonization movement, see ibid.).

[44]

The other, more short-lived colonies of free American blacks which appeared on the West African littoral are often overlooked. Two of these, Mississippi in Africa and Maryland in Liberia, were located on the southeast coast. The former does not concern us here (for more on the Mississippi settlement, see Sullivan 1978), but the latter, sponsored by the Maryland State Colonization Society (MSCS), was planted in the middle of the Glebo town of Gbenelu on the bluffs of Cape Palmas.

The Cape Palmas settlement, which originated in an act of the Maryland legislature in 1832, grew out of both the colonization and evangelical movements of the time and Maryland's peculiar position as a border state (Latrobe 1885:23). In 1810, the state had more "free people of color" than any other in the United States; 38.2 percent of the total population was black, and of that, 23 percent (or 9 percent of the total population) was free. By 1830, the number of those freed had risen to one-third of all blacks or 12 percent of all Marylanders (Martin 1968:55). They were barred from many occupations and seen as a threat by slaveholders and as an uncomfortable reminder of the difficulties of a multiracial society by abolitionists. Their "return" to Africa was the favored alternative of white lawmakers. The Maryland legislature passed bills granting $20,000 in state funds to the American Colonization Society "to apply the means that may be raised in Maryland to the removal of the free people of color of Maryland" (Latrobe 1885:12). The legislature also stipulated that any slave freed in Maryland after passage of the bill in 1831–32 would have the choice of emigrating to Liberia or immediately leaving the state. Although not enforced, the bill was evidence of the increasing hostility toward free blacks which underlay the official philanthropic motives of the American Colonization Society (Martin 1968:56).

In spite of the colonization scheme's popularity among white Marylanders, it was never much admired by it intended subjects. J. Gus Liebenow's figures indicate that between 1831 and 1862, the years of greatest activity by the MSCS, only 1,227 people were settled at Cape Palmas, not all of them from the state of Maryland (1969:8). The lack of recruits from Maryland was consistent with the national trend; only a tiny minority of free blacks seriously considered emigration as anything other than a white plot to get rid of them. Nonetheless, only a year after appropriating funds to the national body, Maryland redirected this money to the local chapter, the MSCS, and requested that it look into founding an independent colony specifically for Maryland's black population. Reasons cited for this move include the belief that the ACS was moving too slowly in exporting colonists from Maryland, that the Monrovia colony was too small for the large number of blacks Maryland would send, and that mismanagement and other abuses were going on at Monrovia. At the urging of the MSCS president John Latrobe, who believed that Cape Palmas would be the key to American commercial exploitation of the newly opened Niger Delta trade, a new site, 250 miles southeast of Monrovia, was chosen for the settlement (Martin 1968:57–58).

Almost from the very beginning, there was a clearly evangelical, missionary component to the MSCS's activities. The flag of the new colony was designed as a replica of the United States flag, but with a white cross rather than stars on the blue field. The motto chosen was the biblical message "Ethiopia shall soon stretch forth her hands to God," and the first colonial agent, Dr. James Hall, was instructed to buy land for the colony from the native inhabitants without including rum or other "ardent spirits" in the purchase price (ibid.:69). The MSCS also offered protection and assistance to the American Board of Foreign Missions with any projects it had planned for West Africa. Later, when the MSCS found itself unable to live up to treaty obligations to provide schools and teachers for the children of both the Glebo and the colonists, it invited the missions to take over all educational matters and granted them land in the colony in return (Earp 1941:367). To the preexisting notions of civilized as well traveled, worldly, and multilingual were soon to be added two more conditions: Christianity and a Western-style education.

The Maryland settlement was unique among Liberian towns in that it was built exactly in the middle of a preexisting indigenous community containing between fifteen hundred and two thousand Glebo (Fox 1868:177). On February 14, 1834, Hall arrived with his first group of seventeen Maryland settlers, plus a few others who had joined at Monrovia and Bassa (Martin 1968:74). In negotiations with three "kings" representing only Nyomowe towns, a treaty was signed granting the MSCS title to roughly twenty square miles of

[46]

territory in return for about $1,000 worth of trade goods (but no rum). It is doubtful that the Nyomowe leaders had any idea of selling their land; rather, they probably viewed the transaction as another trade agreement. Later, they would deny that they ever sold the ancestral town of Gbenelu, within which the colonial town of Harper began to take shape. In any event, the proximity of the two communities on the high bluffs of the cape set the context for the almost inevitable confrontation that was to come.

The MSCS retained control over the colony until 1854, when it became the independent state of Maryland in Liberia. One of the first acts attempted by the new government was to intervene in the ongoing skirmishes between Kuniwe and Nyomowe Glebo and to resolve the tension that had been growing on the cape. The settlers came up with a plan for the "friendly removal" of the Nyomowe of Gbenelu, Wuduke, and Jeploke and their resettlement in the area of the Cavalla River (Kuniwe territory). The Nyomowe refused even to attend such discussions, and Boston Drayton, the governor of the tiny state, responded by turning the settlers' only cannon on the Glebo towns, touching off the war of 1857. While the settlers were on the offensive, they and their Kuniwe allies from Taake and Gbede destroyed eight Nyomowe and allied towns and forced about six thousand people to flee to the interior (ibid.:192–94, 196). A few weeks later, the Nyomowe regrouped and rallied their own allies among interior *dakwe* to cut off the cape from its outlying farms and thus from its food supply. Drayton was forced to appeal to Monrovia for help, and an ACS vessel and an American naval gunboat arrived with supplies and reinforcements just as the colonists were about to be pushed into the sea. With the guns trained on their remaining towns, the Nyomowe quickly came to terms with the invaders.

The treaty that ended the war provided for the resettlement of the Cape Palmas Nyomowe across the Hoffman River near a small village of Christian converts established by the Protestant Episcopal mission. For the site of their former towns on the cape, they were to be paid an additional $1,000 (which they claimed they never received). Finally, the state of Maryland in Liberia was formally annexed to the republic of Liberia as Maryland County in April 1857, after just three years of independent existence (ibid.:201). From that time on, the

[47]

Maryland colony's destiny was interwoven with that of the nation of Liberia, reaching the height of its influence on the national scene during the presidency of native son William V. S. Tubman from 1944 to 1972 (Liebenow 1969:xix).

The Consolidation of State Control

Two processes characterized the history of the region during the second half of the nineteenth century and the early decades of the twentieth. The first was the expansion of the Liberian state from its scattered settler communities along the coast to assume real political control over the territories it claimed. Lands over which the Liberian government was unable to demonstrate effective occupation were quickly lost to Britain and France. In their limited way, the repatriates took part in the scramble for Africa that followed the Berlin Conference of 1888 (Akpan 1973, 1980; Gershoni 1985). The second process was the increasing integration of southeastern peoples into broader economic systems through migrant labor abroad. As the Liberian state attempted to define its borders, these two processes became entwined. Grebo wars were fought in 1875, 1886–1900, 1910, and 1918, often sparked by the government's attempts to control the outward flow of migrant workers and to tax them on their return. Much conflict resulted from the port of entry legislation of 1865, which restricted trading to designated ports coinciding with the old settler communities and administrative centers of Robertsport, Monrovia, Marshall, Edina, Greenville, and Harper (Radke and Sauer 1980:26). Ships which for generations had called at Kru and Grebo towns all along the coast to trade for local products and take on laborers were now technically engaged in smuggling. By this time, the "krooboys" once recruited as deck hands had become essential to the operation of many on-shore operations in the European colonies; they were in particular demand by the palm oil industry in Nigeria, the cocoa plantations of the Spanish island of Fernando Po, and the gold mines of Ghana. Both the laborers and their employers objected to taking private contractual agreements through the Liberian bureaucracy as well as to the customs duties and head fees charged on each laborer ex-

[48]

ported. The British openly suggested that Monrovia "stop med-
dling in the affairs of the Kroo Coast," and some Kru and Grebo
towns went into outright revolt, requesting protection and even
annexation by England (Martin 1982:3–4, 13). Although the British
ignored and avoided Liberian customs regulations whenever they
could, they did not force a confrontation by honoring the requests
with a military occupation.

By the 1920s, the Liberian government was not only in control of
the flow of migrant labor but profiting from it. Individual officials
increased head taxes and customs duties on the migrants and collected a fee for each worker from the ship captains who transported
them. Young men were rounded up by soldiers from the Liberian
Frontier Force and sent off whether or not they were willing to go
(Akpan 1980:101–2, 114–15). Accusations of slave trafficking became so widespread that a League of Nations commission was set
up in 1930 to investigate, forcing the resignation of President C. B.
D. King and seriously threatening Liberian sovereignty. International outrage, much of it genuine, over the abuse of native peoples
was skillfully managed by investors such as Harvey Firestone, who
were devising new uses for Liberian labor at home rather than
abroad (for a full discussion, see Sundiata 1980).

Firestone, the Open Door Policy, and the Development of the Southeast

Following World War I, the British government sought to prop
up falling world market prices for rubber by restricting production
in its Asian colonial possessions. American industries, which at that
time absorbed close to two-thirds of world rubber output, were
outraged by British protectionism and began to look elsewhere for a
supply of rubber that would be "cheap, independent, and guaran-
teed." Among the first to recognize Liberia's potential as a rubber
producer was Harvey S. Firestone of Akron, Ohio, who entered
negotiations with the Liberian government in 1924. In 1927, the
final agreement granted Firestone Rubber a one-million-acre concession area at an annual rent of six cents an acre for a period of
ninety-nine years. Liberia granted the company numerous tax in-

centives and was required to accept a $5 million loan from Firestone to service the national debts to European banks: "It became clear that Harvey Firestone wanted more than just a concession agreement that would satisfy the demand of his industry; he also wanted to have some control over the Liberian Government which owed more than one million dollars to mainly British bankers" (van der Kraaij 1980:200, 203).

The Firestone agreement was only the first of many concessions granted by Liberia to foreign investors. Iron mining in the Nimba Mountains began in the early 1950s, and iron ore eventually outstripped rubber as Liberia's major export (Carlsson 1980:269). Timber, citrus fruit, sugar, and oil palm concessions, although smaller in scale than the Firestone operations, all added to the displacement of subsistence farmers and drew thousands of skilled and unskilled people into the wage sector. Foreign investors were courted with the Open Door Policy of President W. V. S. Tubman: "It is no exaggeration to say that by 1960 Liberia offered private foreign capital one of the more attractive investment climates to be found in the underdeveloped world" (Clower et al. 1966:118).

Yet even at the peak of its economic boom, Clower and his associates could claim, with justification, that Liberia was undergoing "growth without development." Most of the profits made from Liberia's natural resources left the country with the foreign investors; what remained behind was mostly in the hands of the repatriate political elite. Except in a few select concession areas, very little infrastructure was contributed by the foreign corporations, but some did provide schools and medical services for their workers. Thus a new avenue toward civilization, or at least some of the elements associated with civilized life, was opened for native families drawn out of the subsistence sector and into the wage economy. In many cases, wives and children were left behind, and internal male labor migration continued as it had in the era of the seagoing Krumen. But Firestone and the other concessions wanted to establish a stable, year-round labor force; they provided housing for the families of workers and encouraged their employees to reside permanently on the concessions. The workers' wives turned from farming to full-time marketing on the concessions and in nearby towns to fulfill their responsibilities as providers, and their children, no longer needed for farm work, were sent to school. Positions also opened for clerks, accountants, secretaries, and middle-level managers, perfect occupations for men whose families had been civilized for several generations. Whatever their effects might be on the Liberian economy in general, one result of the concessions was to provide native people with an alternative to farming and civilized people with an alternative to government and mission employment. In the process, the size of the civilized population greatly increased.

Liberia, like many African nations, suffered in the world economic recession of the late 1970s; within the country, the southeast was particularly hard hit. The closure of the government sugar scheme, LIBSUCO, which was located about fifteen miles from Harper, threw several hundred people out of work, both administrators and unskilled, uneducated agricultural laborers. The recent shutdown of the Firestone Company's Cavalla River rubber plantation has worsened the employment situation. Many of those who lost their jobs have yet to find new ones in the Cape Palmas area, and each year the four local high schools graduate new classes of educated men and women for whom there is little hope of employment appropriate to their status. Many of these young people gravitate to Monrovia, where, because of government cutbacks, the situation is not much better. Those who have jobs hold on to them tenaciously because a civilized lifestyle requires a regular income. Unemployed civilized men, however, retain their prestige even if reduced to helping their native relatives with farming. Men who find themselves in such a position emphasize that they are not taking up farming as an occupation, only assisting their relatives until an appropriate wage job becomes available.

Christianity and Mission Education: The Spread of Civilization

Although many Christian denominations were represented among both settlers and missionaries at Cape Palmas, the Protestant Episcopal church had the greatest success in converting, educating, and civilizing the Glebo. There are numerous reasons for the church's success: wealthy, upper-class contributors at home;

highly educated personnel, who learned the Glebo language and developed a script for writing it; and a willingness to set up operations in Glebo villages removed from the settler community. Probably unwittingly, they established stations in both Kuniwe and Nyomowe towns, with their principal headquarters at the frequently turbulent Gbede. They had very clear ideas of what they wanted to accomplish: "A good Glebo Christian observed Sunday, pulled down greegrees, and refused to participate in traditional sacrifices, but a good Glebo Christian also wore western clothes, built a western house, married only one wife, and cultivated a garden of flowers" (Martin 1968:212, 206).

This ideal required both an education and gender role training which reproduced nineteenth-century American values. Education was segregated by sex in the mission schools, with classes for girls taught by the wives of missionaries and following a curriculum emphasizing cooking, dressmaking, and homemaking skills (Payne 1845:395). Whereas a native Glebo woman's work centered on the rice farm for which, with the exception of felling large trees and burning, she was primarily responsible, a mission woman's activity was to be restricted to her home, ideally supported by a wage-earning man. This emphasis on gender roles was an explicit policy. Married couples were preferred for missionary work, and C. C. Hoffman, one of the most active of the Episcopal missionaries, recorded his distress at being left in charge of the Girls Orphan Asylum in Harper when his wife died in the field (Fox 1868:231). He quickly remarried on his next home leave.

The missionaries' opinion of the indigenous culture were far from complimentary. The status of women and the economic transactions that accompanied marriage were often cited as examples of Glebo savagery. Bishop Payne, a longtime resident of Gbede, observed: "The natives were as wild as the beasts. . . . The institution of marriage can hardly be said to have existed, for both polygamy and the grossest immorality prevailed. The female children were usually betrothed at six or seven years of age, when the intending husband paid a price to the father, generally consisting of three cows, a goat, and some cloth. When arrived at maturity, without any form or ceremony, the husband took his purchased bride home, and as soon as he could afford it, repeated the process, till he had got as many or more wives than he could maintain" (ibid.:183).

To cope with such practices, the missionaries found themselves having to pay bridewealth to the parents of female children to enroll them in school, a policy the Glebo were quick to exploit (Earp 1941:370). To keep their new converts from backsliding, "the missionaries began the formation of Glebo Christian villages which remained under the control of the mission. By 1865, the village at Cavalla consisted of twelve families or sixty persons. The village of Christian Glebo founded by N. S. Harris among the Cape Palmas people in 1852 numbered about six families in 1858" (Martin 1968:214).

A Salem, Massachusetts, sea captain who visited Cape Palmas in 1840 recorded his observations of the Episcopal mission station at Mount Vaughn, about three miles inland from Harper: "At the foot of the hill or in the valey are hundreths of huts of the Native negroes who cultivate this ground under Mr. Parkinsons own Superintendance. In fact the situation of his house, the extensive Plantation or estate surrounding it, The hamlets of his dependents In the Valley beneath his towering mansion, The extensive view of surrounding scenery. This combination put altogether can scarcely fail of reminding one of one of those Establishments of Feudal times in Europe, and fanceing Mr. and Mrs. Parkins personations of a Lord and Lady of the Manor" (Brooks 1962:165).

What incentives did the missions provide the Glebo to give up their homes, beliefs, and ways of life? Most recruits were young men and boys, who had fairly low status in Glebo society to begin with. Some reportedly attended school just long enough to acquire sufficient English to get Kruman employment on European ships. Those who converted were often suspected by both missionaries and their fellow Glebo of being interested primarily in monetary gain. In the early years, the missionaries made small cash payments in return for attendance at church services and handed out gifts and cash at holidays such as Christmas. Also, converts had priority in trade with the missions, a lucrative business of keeping them supplied with food and building materials. The Salem merchant was more accurate than he knew when he compared the mission station to a feudal village. Most of the residents of these mission towns were employed by the mission, not in farming but in skilled occupations which they learned in its schools and as carpenters, blacksmiths, masons, washerwomen, servants, and the like (Martin 1968:213, 215–17).

An account written by a Glebo historian contends that the Glebo themselves requested missionary teachers from the Maryland State Colonization Society and that they insisted on the provision of schools as conditions of the original treaties signed with the Americans. Samuel Yede Wallace dates the first mission station at Gbede to 1830, four years before the arrival of the colonists (1980:73–74). Other informants agreed that the Episcopal missionaries arrived before the settlers and at the specific invitation of the Glebo, indicating that this interpretation of history is fairly widespread and accepted. Although two missionaries accompanied the original band of colonists in 1834, they represented the Presbyterian, not the Episcopal, church, and there is no evidence that any Episcopal missionaries arrived before 1835 (Fox 1868:181; Earp 1941:368; Martin 1968:73, 127).

The Glebo version of mission history, however, illuminates several important facts. For one thing, just as the Americans encountered two warring groups of Glebo, the Nyomowe and Kuniwe were quick to recognize that they were dealing with two distinct "tribes" among the foreigners: African-American colonists and white missionaries, each with very different motives for being there. Tensions between the two were evident from the beginning as class and doctrinal differences. The missionaries were white, upper and upper middle class, and representatives of established churches, whereas the colonists, some of them only recently freed from slavery, favored the more enthusiastic sects such as the "Jumping Methodists" (Martin 1968:126; Brooks 1962:166). Prejudice and racism were evident on both sides, with colonists fearing that educated Glebo might soon leave them "in the shade" and missionaries feeling that "the influence exerted on the native minds by the vicious and immoral example of the generality of the colonists is a source of very serious discouragement" (Martin 1968:145). Neither side had any scruples about interfering in Glebo political affairs; one early conflict found the missionaries allied with the Kuniwe against the colonists and the Nyomowe. Each of these four powerful factions was involved in a complex game of playing off both sides against the middle, to their own advantage if possible.

[54]

As a result of missionary efforts, however, a fifth group soon emerged, the so-called "civilized Glebo."

> The early policies of the mission tended to isolate a small group of Glebo from both the traditional and Americo-Liberian communities while, at the same time, providing them with an education and encouraging them to emulate western standards often exampled in the Americo-Liberian community. . . . From the time of their emergence as a small group in the 1840's and 1850's . . . the educated Glebo were faced with a continuing problem: how could they best maintain themselves in two communities—the traditional Glebo community and the westernized Americo-Liberian community—which were diverse and conflicting, and to both of which they felt allegiance through birth and training? (ibid.:207, 209)

The dilemma was complicated because despite rhetoric about brotherhood and unity, it was clear that the civilized Glebo would not be allowed to assimilate to full citizenship within the Maryland colony. The unwillingness of repatriates, not just in the southeast but throughout Liberia, to openly incorporate "tribal" people into their privileged minority has been well documented elsewhere (Liebenow 1969; Schmokel 1969). Young Glebo men, whose educational qualifications often surpassed those of most colonists, could not find employment as clerks or accountants in Harper and were referred to as "native dogs." Nor did the missions attempt to alter the situation. The Episcopal congregation of colonists at Harper refused to seat Glebo converts in their church, St. Mark's, but assisted in the construction of a segregated Glebo church, St. James', across the river at Hoffman Station. This most successful of mission towns was itself the result of repatriate prejudice. In 1852, N. S. Harris, a mission-educated Nyomowe Glebo from the town of Kablake, attempted to set up a small school near St. Mark's Episcopal Church in Harper. Hostility from the colonists was so great that he was forced to move across the river and founded Hoffman Station, named after the missionary C. C. Hoffman (Martin 1968:267, 220, 189–90). After 1857, the people of Gbenelu, Wuduke, and Jeploke were also moved across the river to form a solid Glebo community but one divided into natives and mission-educated civilized people.

The Christian Glebo could not rise within the traditional structure of their own society because to do so required ritual sacrifices,
the consulting of oracles, maintenance of community medicines,
and the prosecution of witchcraft through trial by ordeal, all forbidden by their new faith. In addition, status in Glebo society is largely
a function of age, and those recruited by the missions were almost
uniformly young. Finding themselves, in their own words, "on the
way of the bat, we are neither beasts nor birds" (ibid.:209), they set
about creating a role for themselves, in the process laying the
foundation for the present civilized/native division in Glebo
society.

The Liberian Concept of Civilization: Comparative Perspectives

A compelling question is why the same constellation of factors—
missionization, the introduction of Western education, and widespread economic change—did not produce similar distinct civilized
populations elsewhere in West Africa. The immediate answer
would seem to lie in the presence of a large settler population of
repatriated blacks. When viewed in comparison with neighboring
Sierra Leone, settled in 1787 as a depot for the repatriation of free
blacks from England, Canada, and the West Indies, however, the
situation becomes more complex and Liberia's uniqueness is
revealed.

E. Frances White has argued convincingly that Sierra Leonian
Krio (or Creole) culture, which bears a superficial resemblance to
that of the Liberian repatriates, is a product not of the early nineteenth century but of the early twentieth. White's historical research indicates that Krio ethnic identity did not take shape until
much later in the colony's history and that distinctly West African
forms of marriage, kinship, and gender relations dominated during
the first hundred years. As a result, the incorporation of surrounding indigenous people into the Krio category was far easier than the
corresponding process in Liberia (1987:81–82, 10–11).

Some of this difference may be attributed to the smaller number
of highly assimilated repatriates who settled the British colony. In
Sierra Leone, the ratio of American immigrants to "recaptured"

Africans, those taken off impounded slave ships before they crossed the Atlantic, was much lower than in Liberia. Recaptives who landed at Sierra Leone often maintained their identity as Yoruba or Igbo for several generations, possibly because the size of these groups allowed them to form homogenous communities in Freetown. Some were able to reestablish contacts with their home communities down the coast, using these connections as a valuable resource in the growing coastal trade. Through the late nineteenth century, Krio culture was open and flexible enough to allow Christian, town-dwelling women with English names and Krio identities to establish long-distance trade networks and even join indigenous women's secret societies without loss of status. White argues that it was only as British and Lebanese competition eroded the economic base of Krio society, accompanied by a corresponding rise in hostility and racism with the growth of British imperialism, that a thriving Afro-European culture was forced to define itself in purely European terms. This culture was manifest in a new rigidity in marriage forms and increasing restrictions on women's mobility and economic independence, by which the Krio community "demonstrated its distinctiveness, claimed as superiority, from the protectorate peoples and its closeness to the British" (ibid.:26–27, 56, 62–63, 66). White appears to be describing the creation and solidification of a civilized status category such as already existed at this time in Liberia.

In Liberia, of the roughly twenty thousand settlers, only about six thousand were recaptives who had never reached the New World. These recaptives were distributed among the American settlers under a system of wardship and apprenticeship and were thus absorbed within a generation into Liberian colonial society. The leading figures among the American repatriates were drawn from the roughly five thousand who were born free or were manumitted in the United States. Many of these settlers were the offspring of slave mothers and white fathers; they were frequently well-educated property owners and small businessmen and were leaders of the free black communities in their home cities (Liebenow 1987:18, 21). It was this group which defined colonial society in the crucial early years. Between 1820, when the first shipload of colonists left for West Africa, and 1828, all of the immigrants were freeborn. Only after 1828 did the first former slaves begin to arrive (Dunn and Tarr 1988:212, n. 6).

It is significant that Liberia's early settlers brought with them a middle-class, business-oriented, urban culture rather than an African-American background characterized by rural plantation slavery and a strong core of modified West African cultural elements. In contrast, Sierra Leone's first successful settlers, after the demise of a colony of "poor blacks" from London, were the "Nova Scotians," mostly former slaves from plantations in South Carolina and Virginia who escaped to the British during the American Revolution and were resettled temporarily in Canada before immigrating to West Africa. White points out that some members of this group were native-born Africans and all had shared in an American plantation society with well-documented African components. In 1800, they were joined by a group of Jamaican Maroons who had had so little contact with Europeans they had not yet converted to Christianity (1987:8–9, 23). The defining characteristic of the Sierra Leonians, in contrast with the Liberian repatriates, was their openness to the surrounding indigenous peoples.

In other parts of West Africa, some American-born blacks were repatriated, but their numbers were significantly smaller. Individuals who chose to return to the land of their ancestors but rejected the repatriate colonies of Sierra Leone and Liberia may have been motivated by a positive view of Africa and did not hold themselves aloof from the indigenous people. The initial colonists of Liberia, by contrast, had been moderately successful within a middle-class, entrepreneurial, urban setting in the United States. They understood the limits placed on their economic and political ambitions by American racism and were willing to risk resettlement in an area where those ambitions might have free rein. By the time they were joined by the recaptives and the recently manumitted plantation slaves, who might have been more open to assimilation with local peoples, the middle-class repatriates had already defined the complex of values and behaviors known as civilization. Their political and economic ascendancy allowed them to impose their lifestyle as the model for those aspiring to join them.

The second component of Liberia's uniqueness, beyond the origin and number of the settlers, was the issue of race as a central feature in the definition of civilization. It is of crucial importance to keep distinct the different meanings of civilization held by various groups. Although European missionaries and colonial officials held themselves to be agents of the "civilizing mission," by the mid-nineteenth century there was serious disagreement among whites over whether Africans were capable of assimilating Western culture (Berman 1975:7). All over West Africa, educated people who expected to be judged according to universal standards of civilized behavior found themselves rejected and ridiculed by Europeans for whom skin color was the overwhelming measure of value. By 1855 in Ghana, for example, this group was noted with suspicion and disdain: "There is growing up an intermediate class—. . . half-civilised—men with a certain amount of English knowledge and ideas derived from the missionaries or elsewhere" (quoted in Boahen 1974:244).

The effect of European racism in the West African colonies (including Sierra Leone, which did not become independent until the 1960s) seems to have discouraged members of the educated class from completely breaking ties with their families and communities. Because "passing" into the white colonial elite was physically impossible, educated Africans emphasized their common interests with, rather than differences from, the masses of the people. In Liberia, however, independence was declared in 1847, and the white presence before that time had consisted of a few ACS agents and missionaries. Members of the repatriate elite could not base their claims to superiority on biological difference from the surrounding people, nor could they contend that blacks were incapable of becoming civilized, although early political struggles between mulatto and "true black" factions may have represented some attempt in this direction (Dunn and Tarr 1988:48). For the most part, however, repatriate elites had to rely on group endogamy and an almost obsessive concern with individual genealogy to maintain their political and ideological superiority. They also controlled such "gatekeeping" institutions as schools, churches, Masonic lodges, and other secret societies to restrict class and status mobility. Liebenow has documented the dense web of intermarriage which united the uppermost levels of the repatriate elite through the end of the 1970s (1987:102–15). "Outside children" of repatriate men by their "country wives" were, over time, merged into official family histories, augmenting the supposedly endogamous group without challenging the myth of "pure" settler descent.

The Growth of Civilized Towns in the Southeast

Just as mission-educated Africans in Ghana were rejected by Europeans as "half-civilized" on the basis of their race, the educated Glebo of Cape Palmas were rejected by the Harper settlers because of their continuing identification as Glebo. The civilized Glebo, in turn, rejected the definition of civilization offered by the colonists in favor of their own model. The process by which the civilized community emerged in Cape Palmas is not unique in Liberia. Merren Fraenkel has described the development of the civilized Municipality of Grand Cess from the coastal Kru town of Siklipo, to the west of Cape Palmas. The parallels are dramatic:

> The precipitating factor in the separation of the "civilized" population from the Big Town of Grand Cess was not the influence of the Liberian Government, which made little or no attempt to bring the area under its control until the 1920's. In so far as outside influence was responsible, it was that of foreign missionaries, and especially, of the schools they opened. Kru from Grand Cess had been travelling down the coast, and coming into contact with Christianity, before the American Methodist missionaries arrived in Grand Cess in 1889. The missionaries were granted land some distance outside Siklipo, and here they built their mission house and school. However, their activities were regarded with some suspicion by the majority of Siklio, who suspected them of being forerunners of the Government. The Christian converts were generally disapproved of, and sometimes physically maltreated. Eventually, in 1910, the converts moved out. . . . Most of the converts were young men who had been educated at the mission school. They named their first settlement "New York." It was built within sight of Siklipo, on traditional farmland. (1966:163)

In this case, the civilized community emerged without a settler population to serve as a model, completely as the product of indigenous tensions and missionary teaching. The youth and structural inferiority of the disgruntled converts is stressed in Fraenkel's account, but she also mentions their commitment to their *panton* (the Kru term for the Glebo *pano*) identities: "The twenty-nine pioneers of New York were drawn from several different *panton* or patriclans. Most were by now on bad terms with their *panton nyefue*, their clan elder, but they nevertheless retained loyalties to the *panton* and even made an initial attempt to settle New York spatially on *panton* lines" (ibid.:164).

Fraenkel notes that the missionaries seem to have had little to do with the formation of the new settlement and that it was not built around the mission compound. It will be remembered that in Cape Palmas, Hoffman Station was founded not by the missionaries but by a civilized Glebo, N. S. Harris, after an unsuccessful attempt to join the repatriate community in Harper (Martin 1968:189–90). Likewise, the Jlao Kru of Sasstown developed a civilized community after a port of entry, established there in 1909, "accelerated *indigenous* changes which already included reformist movements and a Christian element converted in Lagos" (Tonkin 1981:315). Fraenkel (1966:165), Tonkin (1981:313), and Martin (1968:19–20) have all emphasized the intergenerational conflicts that existed beneath the formal gerontocracy of the southeastern communities. Fraenkel points out that "the separation of the new town from the old not only divided followers of the new religion and the old one, but also divided the younger, educated generation, eager for change, from the traditionalists (1966:164). What distinguishes the Cape Palmas community from those of the Kru Coast is the very early development of the civilized group and the availability of wage labor in and around Harper.

Present manifestations of this historical process include a dual administrative system, by which "surveyed areas form Townships, Municipalities, and Cities. . . . These are 'civilised,' and taxed and administered within the constitution. The rest is Tribal, separately taxed and administered by a hierarchy of chiefs under the effective control of the County Superintendent" (Tonkin 1981:316). The Liberian legal code is likewise composed of statutory and customary bodies of law, which are applied variously depending on the status of the litigants (see Carter and Mends-Cole 1982:157–82 for a full

[61]

discussion). But as Fraenkel notes, "'civilized' is *not* a status actually defined by legislation, comparable to the French *civilisé* or the Portuguese *assimilado*" (1964:67). Thus the system is open for considerable manipulation and negotiation, allowing litigants to claim different statuses depending on whether they believe a statutory or customary court is most likely to favor their case (Tonkin 1981:332).

That a wage economy, by itself, was not a necessary condition for the formation of a civilized element is obvious from the history of Grand Cess: "The fission of the Grand Cess population thus took place during a period when there was little money in the area, and no wage-employment so that economically and materially there must have been little initial difference between the two settlements" (Fraenkel 1966:165). In the 1930s, however, a trading boom on the Kru Coast created a greater divergence between the two communities by creating new jobs for which literacy was a prerequisite. This increasing penetration by a wage economy was typical of the process being repeated all over Liberia during the early twentieth century, stimulated but not sustained by infusions of foreign capital.

In addition to the expanding economy, the expansion of the Liberian state created new, if still limited, opportunities for educated Glebo. Indirect rule as a method of hinterland administration was initiated in Maryland County in 1904, creating positions as interpreters and clerks for illiterate native chiefs (Akpan 1980:96). Once again, civilized Glebo found themselves in an ambiguous position with their loyalties divided between the state and their communities of origin. During the late nineteenth century, the civilized community had remained loyal to and claimed the protection of the government in times of conflict, but by the early twentieth century most educated Glebo were allied with their rebellious native kin. M. B. Akpan argues that, though "at the turn of the century the educated Greboes were at the peak of their allegiance to the national government," the experience of indirect rule had the paradoxical effect of increasing their identification with the sufferings of all indigenous peoples. They were quick to point out, both to the native administration and in publications such as the *Lagos Weekly Record*, that Liberia's "native policy" compared unfavorably with that of the British in Sierra Leone, Gold Coast, and Nigeria (ibid.:104–5, 109). Increasing dissatisfaction with repatriate discrimination and barriers to further political power seem also to have halted the movement toward full assimilation of repatriate values and standards. The civilized Glebo community had defined itself as distinct both from its native origins and from the state. Although they would shift allegiance from time to time according to their perceptions of where their interests lay, the civilized Glebo maintained their indigenous ethnic identity at the expense of a national-level identification.

The Cultural Construction of Civilization

I will now turn to the current Glebo conception of the meaning of civilization and the way it is differentially applied to men and women. The Kru term *kwi* or *kui* has entered Liberian English as indicating civilized, Westernized, or white man's fashion; it is analogous to the Glebo term *kobo de*, civilized life (Innes 1967:53). As an adjective, *kwi* or *kobo* can be applied to food, clothing, manner of behavior, or places; the Glebo today, as in the past, refer to Harper City as *kobo wodo* or white people's town. In her ethnography of Monrovia, Fraenkel comments that the distinction between civilized and tribal "is made, not only in everyday speech, in government publications and in presidential speeches . . . but also in certain legislative enactments" (1964:67). Yet it is not a status which is defined by legislation. The actual application of "civilized" as a status category is open and shifting, defined by a number of aspects: "The most important component of 'civilization' is education, but while to the outsider the question immediately arises of how much education a man needs in order to be regarded as civilized, to the Monrovian it does not occur in quite these terms, since 'civilized' has a much wider connotation than 'educated.' More generally, 'civilized' status involves the adoption of the outward signs of civilized life—Western dress (more especially by the women), house type and furniture. The question the becomes one of how much education a man needs to get a job sufficiently well-paid for him to lead a 'civilized' life" (ibid.:67–68). As Tonkin has noted, there is a certain interactive circularity to this conception: "A salary makes you kui and kuiness is necessary for a salary" (1981:321).

[63]

Fraenkel sees the civilized/native dichotomy as an "embryonic social class structure" in which there is plenty of room for upward mobility through education, employment, and patronage (1964:67, 197). This view stems from the more fluid situation of Monrovia, where the contrast between civilized and native is simply one of many between persons of various class and ethnic backgrounds. The present-day civilized Glebo, it is important to remember, are still very much Glebo. They most definitely do not identify with the repatriate or, in their terms, Congo elite of Harper. What I will be describing here is not so much the construction of the Liberian concept of "civilized" as that of "civilized Glebo," and the distinction is crucial. A Glebo might be described as *misa,* mission, but never as *kobo,* white, or European. As indicated earlier, a Glebo individual, as long as he or she can be identified on the basis of town citizenship and *pano* membership, is a Glebo, no matter what style of life he or she lives.

The Glebo agree that a civilized person is educated (at least minimally literate) and a Christian, but they emphasize that "civilization is different from Christianity." The church has many native members who live a traditional life in all other respects. One point that was almost universally made in discussions of civilization is the emphasis on cleanliness: "In a civilized household, the first thing the people do when they get up in the morning is sweep." This is true; most mornings of my life in the civilized town of Hoffman Station, I was awakened by the sound of numerous brooms, sweeping out not only the houses but the dirt yards on all sides. Although I lived about twenty feet from the supposedly native town of Wuduke, I never noticed a difference between the early morning practice of my native and civilized neighbors. To the civilized people themselves, however, housekeeping standards are an important distinction. Tonkin, in her study of Sasstown, likewise found that "all but one of the respondents defined kuiness especially in terms of cleanliness and proper behavior" (1981:323).

Civilized people also say that they keep their pots and dishes covered to keep the flies off their food. The implication is that civilized people, by virtue of their greater education and sophistication, understand the relationship between flies and disease, although flies are present at all stages of food preparation and cooking. The civilized community also makes use of the services of country doctors, herbalists, and other specialists in traditional medicine, even though these practitioners are natives. It is especially interesting that those features chosen to delineate civilization fall among the responsibilities of women (sweeping, the preparation and presentation of food) according to the sexual division of labor. Women's behavior, therefore, helps to define the civilized status of the entire household.

An individual may become civilized in several different ways, although all include a period of socialization or training. He or she may be born into a civilized family in which both parents are literate and one or both are employed in the wage sector. Children born to such a family will be baptized in the church and sent to school as a matter of course. Since most civilized men have one or more "country wives" or "*lappa* women" in addition to a civilized wife (150 years of missionary work have not yet succeeded in eliminating polygyny), the children of these unions are usually also sent to school and may actually be raised in the father's official household and trained by his "married wife" (see also Fraenkel 1966:168–69 for similar data from Grand Cess). The concept of training encompasses a great many of the notions of cleanliness previously referred to, as well as personal dress and comportment, etiquette, formal education, and religious instruction, all designed to produce a civilized person. There appears to be a strong sense that training for civilization must begin at an early age. Children who are attending school are not considered civilized by default; rather, they have the potential to become so, as long as their education and training are not interrupted for a long period of time. Of Tonkin's forty-nine student informants in Sasstown, all of whom were in the top three high school grades, most considered themselves safely *kui* but eleven felt themselves to be "in between" or "both *kui* and country" (1981:322). In Cape Palmas as well, most young people who are still in school by age fifteen or sixteen seem firmly set on a civilized trajectory. All teenagers in school are not necessarily in the high school grades. Because of the high rate of failure on the Liberian national examinations and the advanced age at which most children start school, there are many eighteen-year-olds in the sixth and seventh grades. Even if they must leave school after achieving only

[65]

the barest literacy, however (as is often the case, because of pregnancy, for girls), they will try to maintain a civilized lifestyle.

Training, which produces civilized individuals and reproduces the behaviors that are recognized as civilized, is another of the duties of a civilized woman. In many households, native children from the interior or from more isolated Glebo towns are placed as foster children or servants, usually through links of kinship or friendship between the parents and foster parents; such children are trained and educated in the same manner as the others. Supervising a large household of children and adolescents, some her own, some her husband's, some related, and some unrelated, is an integral part of the civilized *kaede* (house mother's) domestic work. Aspirants to civilization are trained by carrying out all those housekeeping chores that figure so prominently in the definition of the status position. Since most of these young people are not unambiguously civilized, it is not the performance of this work that alters their status. Rather, it is the internalizing of the value placed on such activities, not the mechanics of doing them, that is learned during training for civilization.

In contrast with the traditional Glebo construction of gender, a civilized man is expected to support his wife and family by his earnings at a wage job. Most well-educated men in this category find employment as schoolteachers or in some aspect of government administration. Since Harper is the administrative center for Maryland County, it is the site of three of the county's four high schools and numerous government and religious elementary schools as well as Liberia's only technical college. Here also is the County Administration Building, housing the debt court, the higher circuit court, the Immigration Service for the nearby frontier with Ivory Coast, and numerous other arms of government requiring clerks, typists, messengers, and so on. The Lebanese business community in Harper also employs a number of men as store clerks and warehouse assistants. The Catholic Mission is a big employer, as are the government hospital, the port, and the airfield. The strategic location of Hoffman Station, connected to Harper by a dirt causeway across the river, makes it convenient for many men to have their homes in the Glebo community and their jobs in the city.

Ideally, the civilized woman is supported by her husband. Some, who have a fairly high level of education (a high school graduate is considered very highly educated in Liberia), are employed as teachers or clerks in the county administration, and a few others are nurses at the hospital. These women have their own careers, and some are independent household heads supporting their children and other dependents by themselves. Most civilized women, however, are not as well educated as their husbands and are not qualified for jobs in the wage sector, even if such were available. These women are, more or less, housewives; they do no agricultural work, with the exception of some kitchen gardening, and status considerations prevent them from going into business for themselves in the public marketplace. Their primary duties are the care of the home and the raising and training of children and servants.

When compared with other cultures, this definition of the civilized woman is not very surprising. Social historians have documented the rise of a "cult of domesticity" (Cott 1977; Ryan 1981), which accompanied the growth of the American middle class during the nineteenth century. The elaboration of housekeeping and child care into a peculiarly women's profession involved a whole complex of ideas about dirt, cleanliness, and the separation of home from workplace. Jonas Frykman and Orvar Lofgren have offered a detailed analysis of the growth of the middle class in Sweden, documenting changes in concepts of time, dirt, home, and the human body from a baseline of the early nineteenth-century peasantry. As the middle class struggled to distinguish itself both from the aristocracy and from the emerging industrial working class, its members imposed upon their world a notion of "bourgeois discipline" (Frykman and Lofgren 1987:221), with an explicit equation between household order and moral order. This concept is recognizable as Mary Douglas's venerable "purity rule" (1966) which requires that higher-status persons exert increasing control over bodily functions and the environment within which the body operates. Differences in cleanliness, or purity, either real or supposed, reflect very real social and economic status differences between households in many societies. Domestic order is both emblematic of the triumph of culture over natural disorder and of the more refined sensibilities of high-status persons.

Yet there appears to be very little difference in the daily domestic practice of civilized and native households. The children and servants of civilized homes begin their day by sweeping, but so do those of their native neighbors. Enamel bowls with covers for keeping off flies are standard equipment in every home, including the seasonal homesteads of subsistence farmers. Women farmers, who are busy with their agricultural work, may have less time and inclination for housekeeping and interior decorating than do civilized women, but successful market women, who are also defined as natives, have homes identical to those of the highest-status civilized families. All Glebo, to my knowledge, bathe scrupulously twice a day. Lack of attention to personal hygiene is taken as a sign of mental illness by both native and civilized people. Indeed, the most common personal item adorning the graves of native, non-Christian Glebo is their galvanized metal bath buckets, indicating a desire to maintain standards of personal cleanliness even beyond this world. The explicit equation between civilization and "cleanly comfort," in Tonkin's words (1981:323), appears to exist at the level of ideology rather than in practice.

A civilized woman is known by the ultimate symbol of her status, Western-style dress. Men of all statuses wear Western clothing as a matter of course; they wrap the traditional cloth around their hips only when relaxing at home or on ceremonial occasions. Traditional garb for Glebo women consists of two lengths of cloth, each about two yards wide, called *lappas,* one wrapped and tucked around the waist and the other likewise under the armpits. In reality, such style of dress is seen only in women's ceremonial dancing, and most women wear a blouse or imported T-shirt over the wrapped *lappa* skirt and use the second *lappa* as a baby carrier or as protection from the rain. A native, uneducated woman does not wear any other type of clothing, even if, like some of the more successful market women, she could easily afford a locally made or imported Western-style dress. The dress is a mark of status reserved exclusively for civilized women and girls. It is not necessary, however, that dresses be worn at all times, once the status of a particular woman is known in the community; many prominent civilized women appear in public in elaborately tailored *lappa* suits or even in the traditional two *lappas,* with no loss of status.

For women, the association between clothing style and status is

[68]

so strong that *"lappa* woman" is used interchangeably with "native" or "country woman." The native, usually nonresident secondary wife of a civilized man is known as his *lappa* wife, and the Episcopal church at Hoffman Station sets yearly dues for its members at three dollars for civilized women and two dollars for *lappa* women, ignoring or masking the variation in access to cash that exists within and between these categories. Men, regardless of status, are charged five dollars a year. The ultimate degradation for a civilized woman is to be forced, through economic necessity, to "tie *lappa* and make market"; those who have been reduced to this are said to be no longer civilized. "She used to be civilized, but now she is in the market" is a common element in women's gossip and a clear reminder that one may suffer a sudden fall from prestige. Of a young girl who had been brought from the interior and placed in a civilized home for training but had to be sent back because of her intractable behavior, one woman said, "I know the next time she comes in town she will be wearing *lappas.*" In other words, the girl had had her chance to move up in status but had lost it. She would never wear a dress again.

It appears that only women can lose their status as civilized by engaging in this type of economic behavior; I never heard it said of a man that "he used to be civilized." Usually, a woman's fall from status is attributed to the loss of a man's wage, either through abandonment, death, or unemployment. Therefore, it would seem that a woman's rank as a civilized person is gained through her relationship to her husband or partner. Yet there are many women who are not securely attached to a man and his income but who cling to their position through an almost clandestine marketing system that employs children and a "back door table" to avoid appearing in the public market. These strategies will be discussed in detail in Chapter 5.

Civilized women are barred from large-scale (and lucrative) marketing by status considerations, and they are also kept from subsistence agricultural production by ideas about women's physical strength and capabilities that differ radically from the native construction. Civilized Glebo women are held to be "not strong" enough to do the hard physical labor that native women carry on routinely. Likewise, they are said to be unable to carry heavy loads

[69]

of wood and water that native women transport on their heads, often over long distances. Since these are basic resources for the household, a civilized woman must depend on the labor of men or, more likely, children and adolescents, to supply her needs. One young civilized woman who was barely holding on, economically, to her status, was engaged in a constant struggle to get her nearby native relatives to help her with wood and water. Her own children were too young to provide the labor, and to have been seen carrying such loads herself would have been detrimental to her position in the community.

That these same civilized women will cheerfully take on tasks that are supposed to be beyond their strength in other contexts does not seem to challenge the basic assumptions. Civilized women often transport loads of dirt and water at communal house-building events and work hard at cleaning the church grounds by cutting bush with a cutlass and hoeing up the grass to make a smooth dirt yard. The inability of civilized women to do such work on a daily basis is sometimes offered as an explanation for the numerous servants in civilized households. In fact, the acquisition of wood and water as well as such subsistence and cash-generating activities as farming and marketing seem, in this context, to be the "key tasks" around which gender constructions are clustered to keep women dependent on men (Bourque and Warren 1981).

Civilized women do not loll about with nothing to do; their work of managing large, complex households without running water or electricity, cooking over wood fires, the continual washing and pressing of children's school uniforms and the other clothing that is so important for maintaining status is, in their words, "not easy." In addition, there are numerous church and community-related activities that require both volunteered labor and cash contributions.

A civilized woman without an employed man, however, is in the unenviable position of being virtually unable to support herself and her children, and there are many in these straits who depend on relatives and boyfriends for a precarious existence. Lack of employment has resulted in the outflow of young men, very often after they have fathered several children, who are left with their economically handicapped mothers. Paradoxically, young men frequently appeal to notions of female self-sufficiency and the traditional image of woman as provider in justifying this situation: "Children do not belong only to the father, the mother must help." But there are very few ways in which these mothers can help themselves.

The intersection of two sometimes contradictory prestige systems, gender and civilization, has resulted in a category of women who, by definition, can retain their status only by remaining dependent on men who are often unwilling to provide for them. In this case, the cultural construction of gender and the accompanying sexual division of labor result in economic and prestige differences between women as well as between women and men (see Bourque and Warren 1981). Civilized women pay for their prestige with dependence, yet they reproduce the conditions of that dependence by training the next generation to conform to the same principles. The prestige system thus rests precisely on the daily practice of those whom it almost severely oppresses.

The obvious question that presents itself is why any Glebo women would want to be civilized. Tonkin offers an answer: "People aspire to civilisation because it is attractive. It attracts my readers. None of us wants to spend our lives in hard manual labour for subsistence, however much we respect the intelligence, courage, and creativity of many who do" (1981:323).

That civilization is seen as a positive situation in spite of the contradictory experience of many women is not, ultimately, surprising. We in this country maintain the fiction that anyone can, by individual initiative, rise from poverty to wealth and power in spite of impressive evidence to the contrary. The fortunate women whose husbands are well employed and the few professional women with careers of their own serve as models of the lifestyle others are striving for. They represent the possibilities of civilization, both for poorer women and for schoolgirls preparing for a civilized life. If one is lucky enough to marry well, to catch the eye of a "big man," the ideal of civilized womanhood can become a reality. Weber's concept of status honor helps to clarify the meaning of civilization in Glebo society: "In content, status honor is normally expressed by the fact that above all else a specific *style of life* can be expected from all those who wish to belong to the circle. As soon as there is not a mere individual and socially irrelevant imitation of another

[71]

style of life, but an agreed-upon communal action of this closing character, the 'status' development is underway" (1946:187–88).

The civilized Glebo in this sense constitute a status group, membership in which is internalized along with other identities based on kinship, language, and town citizenship. Weber says, "In contrast to classes, *status groups* are normally communities. They are, however, often of an amorphous kind" (ibid.:186). What remains to be demonstrated, however, is how women use and manipulate conceptions of civilization to survive in an often hostile socioeconomic system. What impact do these ideas actually have on the everyday lives of Glebo women? The following chapters will address this question as it pertains to three areas: household composition, economic strategies, and participation in community events.

[4]

Settlement, Household, and Status: Civilized and Native Towns

Like individuals, Glebo communities are characterized as either civilized or native. The criteria used to assign entire towns to these categories, however, are not the same as those used to define the status of persons. In the case of communities, the terms *native* and *civilized* are used to contrast the historical depth and physical layout of indigenous settlements and those founded after the arrival of the settlers. The designation of towns as civilized and native, however, also implies the status of their residents; native towns are presumed to be occupied exclusively by natives and civilized towns by civilized people. In fact, my census of the Gbenelu cluster revealed that residence is far less segregated than the application of these terms might suggest. Just as civilization does not automatically bring wealth and ease, residence in a civilized town neither implies nor confers civilized status. A better indicator of civilization would appear to be the structure and organization of the domestic unit, since the census points up clear differences in the composition of civilized and native households. But a particular household structure, the presence of foster children and other dependents, occurs not only among civilized families but in those headed by women who are professional marketeers as well. The determination of a domestic unit's status, therefore, depends on more than its internal composition and place of residence.

In this chapter I will describe the various communities in which this research took place, discuss the ways the terms *civilized* and *native* are applied to residential areas and to households, and analyze the domestic arrangements made by women in various status categories. The data are derived from a house-to-house census which I conducted in 1983 in a cluster of six residential areas locally defined as towns. Two local civilized Glebo women assisted me as translators and research assistants, although I attended and recorded all census interviews by myself. The communities I will discuss fall within the jurisdiction of Harper City (see Figure 4) and are deeply emeshed in its semi-urban economy. The opportunities and life chances of their residents must therefore be viewed in this context.

The last official Liberian census (1974) lists the population of the Harper Commonwealth District at 17,113, and of Harper Municipality at 11,714 (Republic of Liberia, 1976). Both figures indicate a significant increase over the 1962 census (the only other national census of the modern period) of 14.3 percent, with adjustments made for the alteration of census districts between 1962 and 1974 (Hasselman 1979:74). Although there are no more recent figures available, it is evident that Harper has experienced both a population and an economic decline in the past few years, attributable primarily to the closing of a large government sugar-producing scheme in the early 1970s. The mayor estimated the population in 1982 at between 15,000 and 16,000 for the Commonwealth District and roughly 10,000 to 12,000 for the city itself.

The city of Harper acquired a great deal of infrastructure, compared with other locations in Liberia, during the tenure of native son President William V. S. Tubman from 1944 to 1972. Streets were paved in the small downtown area, water and electrical services were installed, the port was expanded, a telecommunications office and radio station were built, and numerous public buildings, including an elaborate city hall, a library-museum complex, and a technical college, were added. Since Tubman's death, much in Harper has deteriorated, and the radio station and telephone system are no longer operational. Water and electricity, dependent on a fuel-oil-powered generator, are erratic or nonexistent because shipments of fuel from Monrovia are unreliable. A few Lebanese merchants own their own generators and so manage to keep their supplies of frozen foods, beer, and soft drinks cold. The repatriate owner of the town's only movie theater/disco also has his own generator.

[74]

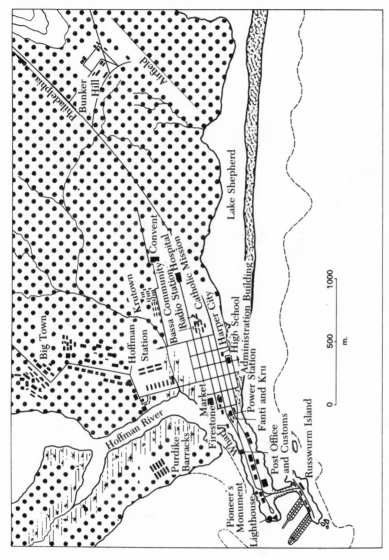

Figure 4. Map of Harper City and surrounding area (from Schulze 1973:76). Reprinted with permission from the Longman Group.

[75]

Illustration 2. View of the city of Harper from the "Up Cape," the original site of Gbenelu, 1982. The present towns of Gbenelu, Hoffman Station, and Wuduke are visible across the mouth of the river.

Harper, like other Liberian cities, is ostensibly divided into specific ethnic enclaves named after their respective "tribes": Old Kru Town, New Kru Town, Bassa Community and so on. The Up Cape and central downtown areas are said to be inhabited by Congo or repatriate families and the families of the Lebanese merchants. All of Harper's neighbors are diverse, both in ethnic and class composition, and the ethnic labels function more as geographic place-names than as a description of settlement patterns. Although many local Glebo live in downtown Harper as well as in the ethnic neighborhoods, there is general agreement that the Grebo Town is across the river in Hoffman Station (see Illustration 2).

Of the six Glebo towns that I call the Gbenelu cluster, four are so contiguous that some residents are not sure in which named locality their house actually stands. Even long-term residents frequently disagree as to which tree or bush marks the boundary. Two other communities are more geographically distinct; Gbenelu is separated from the other towns by a laterite road, and Puduke is located on a swampy peninsula and may be reached only by canoe. The six towns vary widely in size and population, as Table 2 shows.

Gbenelu, Wuduke, Jeploke, and Puduke were the original cluster of Glebo towns which occupied Cape Palmas at the time of American colonization. Gbenelu, Wuduke, and Jeploke were moved to their present location after the 1857 war; Puduke, always separated by water from the colonial settlement, was allowed to remain on its original site. These four settlements are said by the Glebo to be native towns, that is, they are recognized as historically Glebo communities in which persons can hold membership as natal citizens. Thus a Glebo, civilized or native, is said to be from or can "belong to" Gbenelu, Wuduke, Jeploke, and Puduke, but not to Hoffman Station or Harper City. Hoffman Station was a product of the exclusion of civilized Glebo from both settler and native communities. It is referred to locally as either a civilized town or a mission town (in Glebo, *mesa wodo*, "area of a town where literate people live," Innes 1967:73–74), although there is no longer a foreign missionary presence and the clergymen and lay leaders of the St. James Episcopal Church are all Glebo or Nyabo (from the *dako* just to the north). All of the residents of Hoffman Station say that they "belong" somewhere else; "we are all mixed up here" is a frequent saying, which acknowledges the ethnic diversity and lack of distinct *pano* organization characteristic of the civilized town.

Table 2. Population totals by town, 1983

Town	Total	Male		Female		Households
Hoffman Station	1,413	726	(51%)	687	(49%)	166
Wuduke	703	366	(51%)	337	(49%)	80
Jeploke	200	104	(52%)	96	(48%)	21
Waa Hodo Wodo	247	122	(49%)	125	(51%)	35
Gbenelu	219	120	(55%)	99	(45%)	45
Puduke	151	76	(50%)	75	(50%)	20

All of the civilized Glebo of Hoffman Station, some of whose families have been resident there for generations, hold active membership in one or another of the native towns and go "home" often for funerals, ceremonies, and visits. Glebo living in Harper City likewise consider themselves to belong elsewhere. By definition, then, a civilized town can have no natal citizens; it is not organized along *pano* divisions, and it is not under the ritual or civil authority of a *bodio, wodo baa,* or *gbudubo.*

Waa Hodo Wodo (Waa Hodo's Town), the sixth community, presents both the analyst and the Glebo with a dilemma. The settlement was founded in 1974 by a Gbenelu man named Waa Hodo, who overcame fears of witchcraft and built his house on the opposite side of the road linking Hoffman Station with the Tubman College campus. He was soon joined by others, who either rented newly constructed houses or built their own on land claimed through natal citizenship in Gbenleu. It has since become recognized as a town (*wodo*), named in honor of its founder, and in 1983 contained thirty-five households and several partially completed new houses. Waa Hodo Wodo's status is ambiguous; some people consider it an offshoot of Gbenelu and therefore a native town while others point to its high percentage of strangers (non-Glebo Grebo-speakers and Kru) and say it is more like Hoffman Station.

On the map of Harper (Figure 4), the area of my survey is labeled "Hoffman Station" and "Big Town" (the accepted English name for Gbenelu), plus the area that has been erroneously labeled "Purdike Barracks" ("barracks" refers to a temporary army camp once located in that area). The marshy river mouth, the river itself, and a small creek geographically separate all six towns from the city. Although bridges connect Hoffman Station with downtown Harper and Wuduke with Bassa Community, Puduke may be reached only by canoe or boat (see Illustration 3).

The maps of the six individual towns (Figures 5–10) demonstrate the differences in settlement patterns, particularly those between Gbenelu and Puduke on one hand and Hoffman Station on the other. Gbenelu and Puduke are laid out as clusters of households grouped around open public spaces. These open areas are used for funeral dancing, public meetings, and witchcraft trials, as well as for informal socializing. Great emphasis is laid upon keeping these

Illustration 3. The dirt causeway connecting the Glebo towns with the city of Harper. View of Hoffman Station from the causeway, 1983.

areas clear of brush and grass because the health and vitality of a town are thought to be reflected in how "clean" it is of encroaching vegetation. The layout of Hoffman Station, by contrast, reveals a dense pattern of settlement with little public space devoted to community activities. The open areas that appear on the map are used for garden patches of sugarcane or cassava or have been allowed to return to the natural "bush." Most public events in Hoffman Station center around the St. James Church and its affiliated school and graveyard.

Hoffman Station once included only the area immediately surrounding the St. James Church. On the map (Figure 5), one can see that the old mission station now reaches to the very edges of Wuduke and Jeploke, even filling in the unclaimed space between

[79]

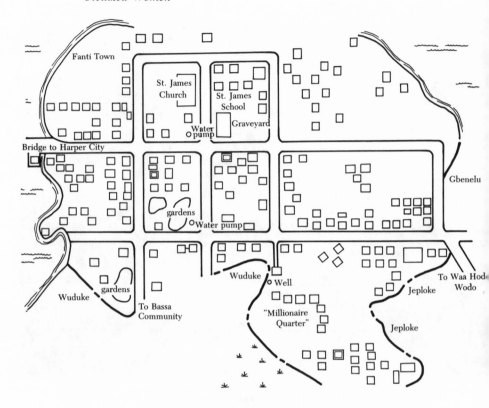

Figure 5. Map of Hoffman Station, redrawn by Imogene Lim from an original by Sao Varmah (not to scale).

them. Once the entire community belonged to the church, but it is now formally a borough of the city of Harper with a chairman elected by the residents under the dual administrative system referred to earlier (see also Fraenkel 1966; Tonkin 1981). Most Glebo, however, still consider Hoffman Station to be part of Gbenelu and occasionally use the two place-names interchangeably. Although regular, laterite roads exist, as on the map, the community is a maze of footpaths and shortcuts, and the neat blocks defined by the established roads have no social significance. The area known as Millionaire Quarter is so called because several prominent and wealthy civilized families live there. According to my census, Hoffman Station had a population of 1,413 people living in 166 enumerated households in 1983. The area labeled Fanti Town was not included in the census because it is occupied by a community of immigrant Fanti fishermen from Ghana. Local Glebo do not consider the Fanti as belonging to Hoffman Station, and the Fanti, who keep to themselves for the most part, seem to concur.

Wuduke (Figure 6), although still considered a native town by the Glebo, is in many ways indistinguishable from Hoffman Station. The home, and therefore the court, of the Nyomowe paramount chief is located here, as is the local office of the Ministry of Public Works. A recently built Pentecostal church attracts primarily non-Glebo Grebo-speakers from interior *dakwe*. The town is connected to the Bassa Community section of Harper by a dirt bridge across a marshy creek, and its proximity to many local schools makes it a popular rental area for students. Since there is at least a remnant of

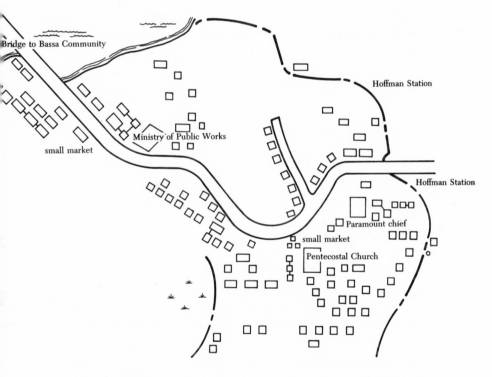

Figure 6. Map of Wuduke, redrawn by Imogene Lim from an original by Sao Varmah (not to scale).

[81]

the original native population still in place, a few of the original *pane* can be defined, but most have been absorbed by newly built rental units for non-Glebo or stranger Glebo immigrants. The town still has its *wodo baa,* or town chief, but he functions primarily as a councilor to the paramount chief and the town chief of Gbenelu. Native activities such as funeral dances still take place in Wuduke, but it is becoming difficult for the dancers to find room to perform among the closely spaced houses. The population at the time of the census was 703 in 80 households.

Jeploke, with a population of only 200 people in 21 households, is dominated by the Big Town Public School, a government elementary school for grades kindergarten through six. The original native town, located directly behind the school (see Figure 7), retains its original *pane* organization to a greater extent than does Wuduke. Tucked into a small pocket between Hoffman Station, Gbenelu, and Waa Hodo Wodo, Jeploke has been less inundated with strangers seeking low rents and proximity to Harper. In appearance, the more dispersed settlement pattern resembles that of Gbenelu and

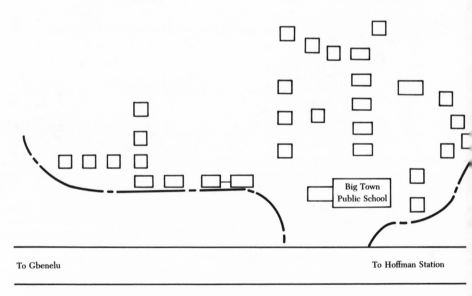

To Gbenelu   To Hoffman Station

Figure 7. Map of Jeploke, redrawn by Imogene Lim from an original by Sao Varmah (not to scale).

[82]

Puduke. Jeploke therefore seems to have more claim to native status than its sister community Wuduke, but census results indicate that natal citizens of the town are in the minority among its residents.

Waa Hodo Wodo is a recent phenomenon. In ethnic diversity and spatial arrangement, it is similar to Hoffman Station and Wuduke, yet, because of its location, it "belongs" to Gbenelu (Figure 8). Most locally born, patrilineally affiliated citizens of Gbenelu, Wuduke, and Jeploke consider Waa Hodo Wodo a stranger town, much like the Fanti community, although a significant pro-

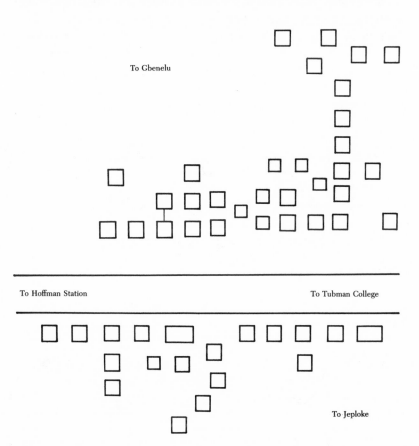

Figure 8. Map of Waa Hodo Wodo, redrawn by Imogene Lim from an original by Sao Varmah (not to scale).

portion of the residents are actually citizens of Gbenelu. As a "town," Waa Hodo Wodo has no real status with the Liberian government and no internal political organization of either the native (town chief) or civilized (chairman) type. The settlement contains 247 people in 35 households.

In contrast with the four contiguous towns, Gbenelu and Puduke are laid out according to *pane* subdivisions. Puduke, the only one of the six towns that is physically separated by water from the others, is located in a coconut grove on the Atlantic coast on the opposite side of the mouth of the Hoffman River. It is the smallest of the six, with 151 people in 20 households. Houses are widely dispersed with large public spaces between them (see Figure 9). Puduke maintains the traditional Glebo political structure with active male age grades, male and female council of elders, and young girls' dancing groups. Traffic across the river to Gbenelu an Harper by

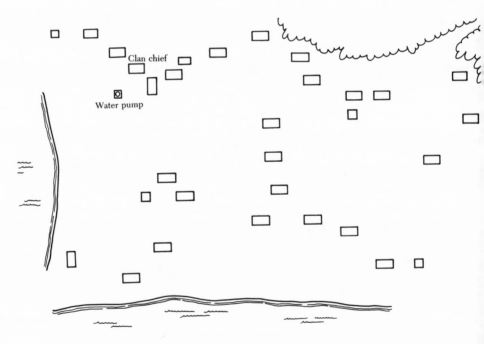

Figure 9. Map of Puduke, redrawn by Imogene Lim from an original by Sao Varmah (not to scale).

[84]

canoe is fairly constant, and many Puduke women regularly sell their crops in the Harper City market.

Gbenelu, the "capital" of the cluster of towns, is also the ritual center and site of the *takae* for Wuduke, Jeploke, and Puduke. The *bodio* and *gyide* occupy the fenced-in structure (Figure 10) and perform the rituals that ensure the health and well-being of the affiliated towns. Like the other four contiguous towns, Gbenelu has been wired for electricity and has a centrally located public faucet to provide drinking water. These services are rarely operational, however, and such minimal infrastructure does little to distinguish Gbenelu from other Glebo centers such as Taake, Waa, Blegye, or Gbede.

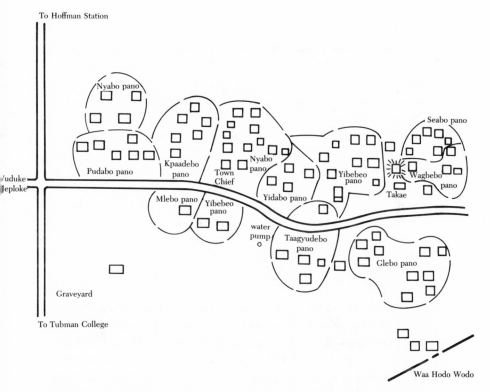

Figure 10. Map of Gbenelu, redrawn by Imogene Lim from an original by Sao Varmah (not to scale).

Demographic Patterns

Fraenkel noted in her study of the Kru Coast that in the 1960s, the native town of Siklipo was steadily losing population to its civilized offshoot, the Municipality of Grand Cess: "The 'Big Town' is big today only in terms of sentiment." At that time, the native Big Town had a population of about 500 to the Municipality's 1,400. A major source of this population drain was that "children are often sent to be brought up in the houses of more educated or wealthy relatives" (1966:157, 168). Similar processes, continuing today in Cape Palmas, have likewise affected the distribution of the population across the six towns.

As I have mentioned, the six towns together are sometimes referred to collectively as Gbenelu and are considered by many to constitute a single Glebo community. Among the four towns that are designated as native, this collective identity is reinforced by reciprocal ritual obligations concerning funeral dancing and by the position of the *bodio* at Gbenelu as the ultimate ritual authority for the area. The Nyomowe paramount chief at Wuduke is the highest legal and civil authority for those who consider themselves natives, and his presence further unites the community. Under the dual administrative system, civilized people are not subject to the chief's authority, yet he is widely respected and referred to as "our king" by civilized and native alike.

The population pyramids shown in Figures 11 to 17, displaying the demographic composition of the Gbenelu cluster as a whole and of the six towns individually, are provided as evidence that the civilized/native dichotomy is more than simply a system of abstract categories. People actively strive to attain and maintain civilized status for themselves and their children, and this effort is reflected in the internal structure of the six communities as well as in the variation in household composition. Figure 11 displays the population distribution of the Gbenelu cluster as a whole, broken down by five-year intervals and by gender. All things being equal, one might expect the populations of all six individual towns to approximate this basic shape. As may be seen from the individual town pyramids, however, this is not the case. Whereas Hoffman Station, Wuduke, Jeploke, and Waa Hodo Wodo have population distribu-

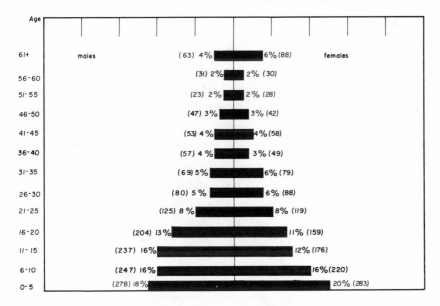

Figure 11. Age pyramid by five-year intervals, total cluster population, 1983. Prepared by Alan Leveillee.

tions which are similar in shape to the population as a whole, Gbenelu and Puduke are considerably different (Figures 12–17).

Both Gbenelu and Puduke seem to be experiencing a loss of young people in the age groups eleven to fifteen (and, for Gbenelu, the age group six to ten as well). Liberia as a whole has very high infant and child mortality, which occurs most heavily between birth and the age of five years (Handwerker 1983). Therefore, mortality alone cannot account for the lack of preadolescent and adolescent children in the native towns. The population pyramids for Hoffman Station, Wuduke, Waa Hodo Wodo, and Jeploke (Figures 14–17), show the bulk of the population concentrated at the lower end of the pyramids, with the school-age population (ages six to twenty-five) making up a very large part of the total.

What might explain the variation in population distribution across the six towns? Access to civilized status is regulated by formal education, which, in theory, is available to all the children of the Gbenelu cluster. A large number of schools, both government (which charge no tuition) and private or church affiliated, are within

[87]

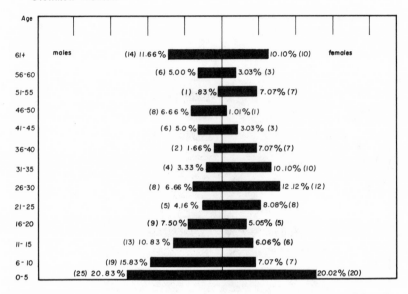

Figure 12. Age pyramid by five-year intervals, Gbenelu, 1983. Prepared by Alan Leveillee.

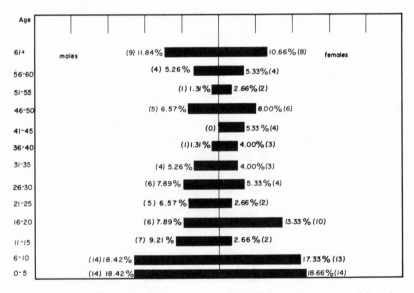

Figure 13. Age pyramid by five-year intervals, Puduke, 1983. Prepared by Alan Leveillee.

[88]

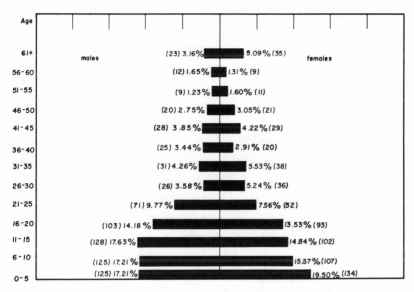

Figure 14. Age pyramid by five-year intervals, Hoffman Station, 1983. Prepared by Alan Leveillee.

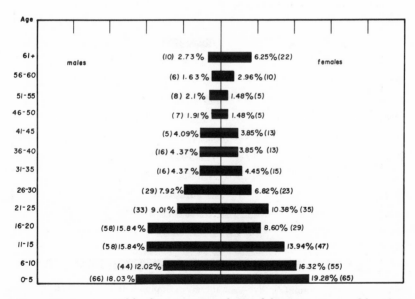

Figure 15. Age pyramid by five-year intervals, Wuduke, 1983. Prepared by Alan Leveillee.

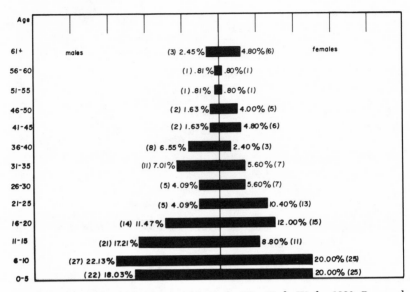

Figure 16. Age pyramid by five-year intervals, Waa Hodo Wodo, 1983. Prepared by Alan Leveillee.

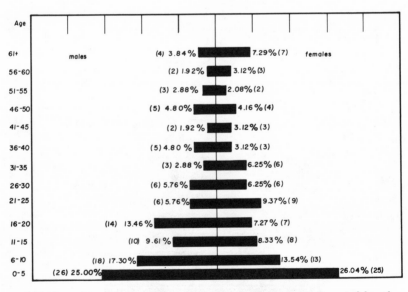

Figure 17. Age pyramid by five-year intervals, Jeploke, 1983. Prepared by Alan Leveillee.

easy walking distance of all these communities except Puduke, which is isolated by water. Even the government schools, however, require a significant investment in registration fees, uniforms, books, and supplies, as well as the loss of the child's labor during the school year. Further, many native Glebo spend most of the year on their farms in the interior, where schools are practically nonexistent. In addition, the cultural construction of civilization stresses not only education but training in the proper conduct of civilized life. This training, it is generally agreed, must begin at an early age to be effective; I do not believe the Glebo could conceive of anyone becoming civilized after the age of fifteen or so. Many of the children missing from Gbenelu and Puduke, therefore, are living as foster children in the other towns of the cluster, attending school and receiving training in civilized life. Even for those young people past the age of acquiring civilization, the native towns and agricultural labor may be less attractive than the search for work closer to Harper. Of the Siklipo, Fraenkel says, "Nobody told me that he had moved, or wished to move, to escape family and *panton* obligations. . . . But some, especially the young people, consider that the Municipality offers more privacy, less restraints, more chances of 'getting on'" (1966:168). Table 3 shows the number of children between the ages of six and twenty-five resident in each town and their enrollment (or lack thereof) in school. The table also demonstrates the unequal proportion of males and females in the student population.

Table 3. School attendance by the population aged 6 to 25

Town	Males enrolled in school		Males not enrolled in school		Females enrolled in school		Females not enrolled in school		Total resident school-age population	
Hoffman Station	50%	(387)	5%	(40)	33%	(264)	12%	(90)	100%	(781)
Wuduke	50%	(180)	4%	(13)	26%	(94)	20%	(72)	100%	(359)
Jeploke	53%	(45)	4%	(3)	22%	(19)	21%	(18)	100%	(85)
Waa Hodo Wodo	41%	(54)	10%	(13)	31%	(40)	18%	(24)	100%	(131)
Gbenelu	22%	(16)	42%	(30)	4%	(3)	32%	(23)	100%	(72)
Puduke	0		54%	(32)	0		46%	(27)	100%	(59)

Gbenelu is the only town in which the percentage of children enrolled in school is smaller than the percentage of those who are not, for both males and females. Puduke has no resident children who are enrolled in school because of the physical barrier of water which separates it from the schools of Harper and Hoffman Station. Although a number of children attending school belong, patrilineally, to Puduke, they are all residing with families in other towns and return to their natal households only during school vacations.

What is important here is the relationship between the towns as child-givers and child-receivers. The children from native towns are placed, usually with relatives, in civilized households for formal education and training. Although not all will emerge as full-fledged civilized people, a significant number will be recruited into this status category as adults. For civilized women, it is children such as these, often related, who constitute the labor force they require to maintain their status. The domestic contribution of this young population keeps the civilized household in wood and water, upholds the standards of cleanliness, and allows civilized women to participate indirectly in marketing. At least one or two children, and often many more, who are not the biological offspring of either the male or female household head are present in almost every civilized home.

The midsection of the age pyramids indicates that the population of those in their thirties and forties drops off sharply. This constriction of the middle-aged groups is less noticeable in Gbenelu and Puduke. Jeploke and Waa Hodo Wodo appear transitional between the blocklike shapes of the Gbenelu and Puduke diagrams and the regular pyramid forms that characterize Hoffman Station and Wuduke. I would suggest that the narrowing of these age groups reflects the out-migration of educated, civilized people from the economically depressed Cape Palmas region to Monrovia and other areas of Liberia. The loss seems to be relatively equal for both males and females. At the very top of the pyramids, Gbenelu and Puduke seem to have a larger percentage of the population that is over age sixty, which may indicate that the migration from Cape Palmas is permanent, or, alternatively, that return migrants retire to their towns of natal citizenship.

We might now wish to question the validity of the Glebo identification of Wuduke and Jeploke as native towns because they seem to share more demographic characteristics with Hoffman Station and Waa Hodo Wodo than with Gbenelu and Puduke. I suggest that the crucial difference for the Glebo is that patrilineal affiliation was and is possible with Wuduke and Jeploke, not possible with Hoffman Station, and possible with Waa Hodo Wodo only insofar as it is considered a part of Gbenelu. This emphasis on patrilineally ascribed citizenship is so great that it overrides other factors, including the present proportion of Glebo to non-Glebo who actually reside in Wuduke and Jeploke (Table 4).

Although everyone in Hoffman Station is assumed to be from somewhere else, ideally the only resident strangers in a native town should be in-marrying wives from other towns and *dakwe* (in Gbenelu and Puduke, the proportion of female strangers is much higher than that of males). The Glebo know that migrants from Nyabo, Jabo, Webbo, Trembo, Boa, and other *dakwe* are increasingly settling in Wuduke, but this does not alter their categorization of it along with Gbenelu and Puduke, where resident strang-

Table 4. Citizenship by town and sex

	Hoffman Station	Wuduke	Jeploke	Waa Hodo Wodo	Gbenelu	Puduke
Males						
Natal	0	18%	33%	19%	79%	93%
citizens		66	34	23	96	71
Other	49%	41%	20%	38%	8%	7%
Glebo	357	151	21	46	9	7
Non-Glebo	51%	41%	47%	43%	13%	0
	369	149	49	53	15	
Total	100%	100%	100%	100%	100%	100%
	726	366	104	122	120	78
Females						
Natal	0	8%	20%	15%	64%	56%
citizens		28	19	19	63	42
Other	53%	50%	27%	37%	25%	43%
Glebo	367	169	26	46	25	32
Non-Glebo	47%	42%	53%	48%	11%	1%
	320	140	51	60	11	1
Total	100%	100%	100%	100%	100%	100%
	687	337	96	125	99	75

ers are relatively rare. The Glebo surely recognize that the pace of life is different in Wuduke than in Gbenelu, that it is fully occupied year-round and contains a high percentage of renters, students, and civilized people. These factors, however, do not transform Wuduke into a civilized town like Hoffman Station or the Municipality of Grand Cess described by Fraenkel. As long as children born to fathers holding Wuduke citizenship continue to belong to Wuduke, the town will remain native in Glebo eyes.

Patterns of Occupation

We have seen that for individuals, the concept of civilization is closely associated with occupation, to the extent that some occupations (farmer, marketeer) cause some civilized people (women) to lose their status. Fraenkel's Kru informants also used occupation as a way of distinguishing between civilized and native towns: "Big Town people live mostly on fishing, farming, and cutting piassava' explained one schoolboy in an essay, 'and Municipality people depend mostly on monthly cheques'" (1966:169). Although this contrast between self-employed agricultural production and dependence on a government payroll applies to such native towns as Gbenelu and Puduke, it clearly does not reflect the situation in Wuduke or, to a large extent, in Jeploke (Tables 5 and 6). In addition, the presence of farmers in Hoffman Station and Waa Hodo Wodo dispels the notion that these historically more recent settlements are entirely composed of wage earners.

The category "Professional" on Tables 5 and 6 includes occupations for which a comparatively high level of education and/or specialized training is required: teachers, county administrators, clerks, medical personnel at the hospital, and members of the Harper police force and fire brigade are all examples. "Laborer" encompasses those working for wages at jobs that require little or no education and training. Of those men who reported their occupation as "the market," one is a government-employed market supervisor and the rest are immigrant Mandingo traders who make up the majority of male marketeers in Harper. The category of "Self-employed craftsman" includes carpenters, tailors, and makers of

Table 5. Occupations of the male population, age 26 and over

Occupation	Hoffman Station	Wuduke	Jeploke	Waa Hodo Wodo	Gbenelu	Puduke
Farmer	8%	19%	37%	18%	76%	90%
	13	20	11	6	37	27
Professional	30%	18%	13%	24%	2%	0
	52	19	4	8	1	
Laborer	19%	21%	13%	24%	6%	0
	35	23	4	8	3	
Market	2%	2%	3%	0	0	0
	3	2	1			
Retired or disabled	7%	7%	7%	6%	6%	3%
	12	8	2	2	3	1
Driver	3%	1%	7%	3%	0	7%
	5	1	2	1		2
Unemployed	15%	20%	10%	18%	2%	0
	28	22	3	6	1	
Self-employed craftsman	10%	5%	7%	6%	6%	0
	17	5	2	2	3	
Religious specialist	1%	0	0	0	2%	0
	1				1	
Chief	0	1%	0	0	0	0
		1				
Fisherman	3%	0	0	0	0	0
	5					
Student	2%	6%	3%	0	0	0
	3	6	1			
Total	100%	100%	100%	100%	100%	100%
	174	107	30	33	49	30

fish traps, cassava graters, brooms, and mats. "Religious specialist" includes native ritual authorities like the Gbenelu *bodio,* midwives, herbalists, and *diobo,* as well as clergy of the various Christian denominations. The category of "Chief" differentiates the Nyo-mowe paramount chief in Wuduke from the *wodo baabo* of the surrounding towns. Both the paramount chief and the town chiefs receive a government salary, but all the *wodo baabo* reported their primary occupation as farming. Neither the paramount chief nor his wives, who are marketeers, are presently involved with agri-culture, and he devotes full time to his judicial and administrative duties.

On Table 6, occupations for women are seen to differ slightly from those of men; the category of "Driver" (of taxis and transport

[95]

Table 6. Occupations of the female population, age 26 and over

Occupation	Hoffman Station	Wuduke	Jeploke	Waa Hodo Wodo	Gbenelu	Puduke
Farmer	5%	29%	26%	25%	75%	100%
	10	30	9	9	40	34
Professional	11%	3%	3%	3%	0	0
	22	3	1	1		
Laborer	2%	1%	0	0	0	0
	5	2				
Market	21%	20%	15%	25%	8%	0
(full time)	41	21	5	9	4	0
Market	7%	3%	0	8%	0	0
(at home)	14	3		3		
"At home" or	49%	39%	56%	36%	15%	0
retired	97	41	19	13	8	
Unemployed	3%	0	0	3%	0	0
	6			1		
Religious	1%	4%	0	0	2%	0
specialist	1	4			1	
Student	1%	1%	0	0	0	0
	2	2				
Total	100%	100%	100%	100%	100%	100%
	198	106	34	36	53	34

trucks), for example, does not appear to be open to females. Most jobs in the "Laborer" category which are available to women are in domestic service with wealthy repatriate or Lebanese families in Harper or janitorial positions in schools and office buildings. Besides public marketing, a number of women have set up market tables in front of their houses or in small groups by the roadsides. Here, they retail the same items, mostly domestic or imported foodstuffs, as are sold in the public market in Harper. This form of home marketing must be sharply distinguished from the "back-door" selling that is carried on by many civilized women; all of the women in the "Market (at home)" category are considered native, and most were previously professional marketeers in Harper. None of the civilized women who were involved in small home businesses, as will be described in Chapter 5, reported this as an occupation on my census. Rather, they reported themselves as "at home," the category that contains the largest percentage of women in Hoffman Station, Wuduke, Jeploke, and Waa Hodo Wodo. The lack of paid jobs available to women in the Harper economy has, of course, important implications for those attempting to maintain civilized status in the absence of an employed husband or lover.

The distribution of occupations across the six towns points to important differences between them, particularly when considering the extremes of Hoffman Station on one side and Puduke on the other. Puduke and Gbenelu seem to fit the local ideal of a native town's economy; Wuduke and Jeploke do not. The use of categories such as civilized and native to characterize communities masks the complexity of people's practice as they strive to become or remain civilized; it is possible for an individual to change his or her status from native to civilized without leaving the town of Wuduke or any other so-called native town. In fact, Wuduke itself has become a major civilizing center, in spite of its label as native.

Household Composition

Along with towns and individuals, domestic units may also be considered civilized or native, depending primarily on the occupation of the male or female head. Tables 7 and 8 provide the occupations of household heads, with those holding professional jobs considered unambiguously civilized. Most men in the "Laborer" or "Driver" categories are not civilized, although some certainly are.

Table 8 contains occupational categories of women who listed themselves as the only heads of their households; in other words, with no resident male head. Some "households" spread themselves over more than one physical structure, sometimes separated by a considerable distance. During the census interviews, the determination of who was considered part of the household was left to the male or female heads themselves. Women who were long-term secondary wives listed themselves as household heads and rarely included their nonresident husbands as household members.⏐That so many of these women list their occupations as "at home" is indicative of their inability to find employment in the wage sector and their dependence on nonresident husbands and lovers.⏐The presence or absence of a resident male head is often crucial to a

[97]

Table 7. Occupations of male heads of households

Occupation	Hoffman Station	Wuduke	Jeploke	Waa Hodo Wodo	Gbenelu	Puduke
Farmer	8%	24%	46%	20%	74%	94%
	9	13	8	6	28	16
Professional	36%	22%	6%	23%	3%	0
	43	12	1	7	1	
Laborer	19%	22%	12%	23%	7%	0
	23	11	2	7	3	
Market	2%	0	6%	0	0	0
	2		1			
Retired or	7%	5%	6%	3%	7%	6%
disabled	9	4	1	1	3	1
Driver	3%	2%	6%	3%	0	0
	4	1	1	1		
Unemployed	11%	18%	12%	20%	3%	0
	13	11	2	6	1	
Self-employed	11%	5%	6%	8%	3%	0
craftsman	13	4	1	2	1	
Religious	1%	0	0	0	3%	0
specialist	1				1	
Chief	0	2%	0	0	0	0
		1				
Fisherman	2%	0	0	0	0	0
	3					
Total	100%	100%	100%	100%	100%	100%
	120	57	17	30	38	17

civilized woman's ability to maintain her status. Female-headed households also vary across the six towns in accordance with the civilized/native dichotomy (Table 9).

Linguistically, the Glebo recognize both a male and a female head of each house (the *kaebuo* and *kaede,* or house father and house mother, respectively). This is consistent with the cultural construction of the genders as essentially separate and noncomplementary. A household managed by a single, independent woman, however, was technically impossible in the native context. Widows were and still are inherited by their husband's male *pano*-mates or are quickly remarried to another man willing to refund the bridewealth paid by the *pano* of marriage. Elderly widows usually remain in their husband's house, preferably under the protection of

Table 8. Occupations of female heads of households

Occupation	Hoffman Station	Wuduke	Jeploke	Waa Hodo Wodo	Gbenelu	Puduke
Farmer	0	36% 8	0	20% 1	57% 4	100% 3
Professional	14% 6	5% 1	25% 1	20% 1	0	0
Laborer	6% 3	0	0	0	0	0
Market (full time)	30% 14	5% 1	0	20% 1	14% 1	0
Market (at home)	14% 6	9% 2	0	0	0	0
"At home" or retired	32% 15	40% 9	75% 3	20% 1	29% 2	0
Unemployed	2% 1	0	0	20% 1	0	0
Religious specialist	2% 1	5% 1	0	0	0	0
Total	100% 46	100% 22	100% 4	100% 5	100% 7	100% 3

an older son. Never-married women managing their own households of dependents are a phenomenon of the civilized towns, although not all such women are civilized. A number of these single women are considered married in the native manner (through the payment of bridewealth) but do not reside with their husbands;

Table 9. Male- and female-headed households, by town

	Hoffman Station	Wuduke	Jeploke	Waa Hodo Wodo	Gbenelu	Puduke
Male-headed	72% 120	73% 58	81% 17	86% 30	84% 38	85% 17
Female-headed	28% 46	27% 22	19% 4	14% 5	16% 7	15% 3
Total	100% 166	100% 80	100% 21	100% 35	100% 45	100% 20
Widows*	45% 20	68% 15	50% 2	20% 1	100% 7	100% 3

*Percentage of female household heads who are widowed.

[99]

they are the *lappa* wives of men who have already married one wife under the formal legal system. Alternatively, they may be truly single women who have profitable market businesses and consider themselves finished with "man business" once they have borne their desired number of children. Still others may be young women who are "loving to" men not ready or able to move in and set up housekeeping with them. Finally, there are childless women who are, indeed, single in that they may be alone, lonely, and even shunned as witches.

The distribution of female-headed households across the six towns demonstrates this pattern, although the low incidence of such households in Waa Hodo Wodo is surprising. Although Waa Hodo Wodo has the lowest percentage of female-headed households, only one of these women is a widow. Waa Hodo Wodo also has the highest percentage of women who are full-time marketeers. In Gbenelu and Puduke, all of the female heads are elderly widows, some with "husbands" assigned to look after them (but not coresident) by the *pane* of their late husbands. The process by which a woman becomes the single head of a household and the implications for her status are clearly different in the civilized and native communities.

It would be very difficult to construct a typology that could capture the range of variation between households in the Gbenelu cluster. Almost half of all farming households consist of a married couple (sometimes polygynous) and their children; the classic composite nuclear family. Yet in households headed by wage earners or marketeers it is not unusual to find, in addition to a nuclear family, both matrilateral and patrilateral relatives of both spouses, more distantly related persons of the "same family" (*pano*), renters, unrelated foster children who are classed as "servants," live-in lovers of older sons and daughters, and unrelated persons who are described simply as "staying here." The majority of these persons in my sample tend to be children or teenagers, younger brothers and sisters of the spouses or children of the spouses' siblings, cousins, grandchildren, and so on. These young people constitute the domestic labor force which both native and civilized women have at their disposal.

The majority of those in all six towns who are not living with their families of origin are living with people they define as relatives. Complementary filiation extends this term to cover a number of matrilateral and matrilineal relationships; genealogical knowledge appears greater in width than in depth. Yet there are some, particularly young people attending school, who either have no civilized relatives living in the vicinity of Harper or who, for whatever reason, cannot find a place with a related family. Those with independent resources or wealthy sponsors may rent a room, alone or with others, and cook for themselves, with a group of friends, or contract for meals with a nearby woman. Few, however, can afford both room and board along with the tuition and fees charged by the schools, and part-time jobs are rare or nonexistent. It is primarily this group, both males and females, who make up the small but significant category of "servants."

Servants may be considered as simply older, usually unrelated, foster children of the household heads. They typically use kin terms as forms of address with other household members and are rarely treated any differently from other young people in the household. All young people, including the biological children of the household heads, are expected to carry out the heavy labor of the household and to wait deferentially on their elders. In return for their work in the home, under the direction of the female head, servants are provided with food and a place to sleep. Few servants receive allowances for clothing or school supplies or have their tuition paid by the host family; such support is expected to come from their own families or sponsors. Most servants tend to be non-Glebo teenagers who have completed primary school in their home areas and come to the coast to continue their education, but some are of local origin and are raised from infancy by their host family.

The term *servant* seems to refer more to the lack of a kin relationship between the person and the household of residence than to a condition of servitude as it might be understood in other contexts. It is clear that *servant* refers to the relationship with the host family rather than the type or quantity of the work expected, since I have heard children as young as two years called servants. Being a servant to a Glebo family is furthermore not considered a job or a lifelong condition; in no case that I know of was a servant not also a student, aspiring to the future rewards of education and civiliza-

[101]

tion. In fact, I was explicitly told that it would be shameful to keep a servant at home, "cooking," while one's own children were sent to school. Although some adult women and men do work as domestics for Lebanese and repatriate families in Harper, this is viewed as paid employment and is significantly different from the servants I have been discussing here. Although small in numbers, the servants represent an option for women seeking additional domestic labor, especially if their own children are all very young of all of one sex. I often heard that so-and-so was "looking for a big girl" or "big boy" (teenager) to fill specific gaps in the household labor force for cutting wood or washing clothes. Often the birth of a new baby prompts a family to bring a teenaged girl into the household; if none are available among their relatives, they will ask about for a servant.

Case Studies

To illustrate further the differences in the internal composition of households, I have provided four case studies, two male-headed and two female-headed households, one each of the civilized and native variety.

Male-Headed, Native. This household is located in Gbenelu. The male head was fifty years old in 1983; like many older Glebo men, he knows the exact year of his birth, which was 1933. He is a natal citizen of the town of Gbenelu and was born there. His wife, aged about thirty-five, is also a natal citizen of the town; at marriage, she moved across town from her own *pano* to her husband's. They have three daughters and two sons, ranging in age from nine years to four months. The couple and their five children are the only residents of the house.

The male head describes his occupation as a rubber and sugarcane farmer; the female head gives hers as a rice and cassava farmer. None of the children are attending school and the two older ones (aged nine and seven) help with the farm work. The family spends most of the year in their farm village in the interior, but the woman has a cassava garden on land belonging to Gbenelu along the road to Tubman College, past Waa Hodo Wodo. Her cassava can be more easily transported into the market at Harper from there than from the interior farm. Both husband and wife are members of the band society (*kumli*) which ensures, in return for the lifelong payment of dues, an elaborate funeral complete with a brass band. The wife also holds the position of *maasan*, the women's dance director, and is widely admired for her skill in dancing. Neither belongs to any Christian denomination and neither speaks Liberian English well enough to feel comfortable in this language. Their house in Gbenelu is small and modestly furnished, but it has a zinc roof like most other houses in town. In sum, they are a fairly typical native family whose agricultural labor provides for all of their subsistence and cash needs and who are deeply involved in the life of the native community.

Male-Headed, Civilized. This family lives in Hoffman Station, very close to Wuduke, of which the male head is a natal citizen. The man is sixty-four years old and is self-employed as a carpenter. He was born in Wuduke, is an active member of the St. James Church, and participates in its men's society. He and his wife, a Kuniwe Glebo woman from Gbede, were married many years ago in a church ceremony. The wife, who is fifty-six, was raised "from small" in Hoffman Station and "trained" by an elderly woman who is still living nearby. This foster mother of the wife had married into the *pano* of the male head of this household; the spouses were in effect raised in the same "quarter" although they are unrelated. The female head describes her occupation as "the house" but adds that she has a small cassava garden for consumption by the family.

The oldest daughter of the couple (aged twenty-seven) has three children of her own (aged nine, two, and five months), all of whom live in the household; her second child is the son of a Lebanese merchant from Harper. This daughter is attempting to finish her education by attending night school; she is currently "loving to" a man from western Liberia who works in town and is the father of her youngest child. He visits frequently but does not reside in the household. Other children, in addition to the daughter and the grandchildren, are the couple's thirteen-year-old son and two sons, aged twelve and fourteen, of the husband by his *lappa* wife. The *lappa* wife, whom the married wife refers to as her "mate," lives on

[103]

the other side of Hoffman Station with several younger children of the male head. As these children become older, he will bring them into his household so they may be trained properly as civilized people. The *lappa* wife sells in the market in Harper.

In addition to the children and grandchildren, there are other related children in the household. These include the man's niece (sister's daughter), age nineteen, his grandnephew (sister's son's son), age twenty-three, a more distantly related fifteen-year-old girl (father's sister's son's daughter), and another grandnephew (sister's daughter's son), age four. All except the four-year-old and the youngest grandchildren are in school. The entire family attends the St. James church and are involved in its activities. The total number of persons in this household is fourteen.

Female-Headed, Native. This household is in Wuduke and is headed by a widow from Puduke who "married to" Wuduke as a young girl. She is about sixty-three years old and does part-time marketing, both at the General Market in Harper and at a table set up by her front door. Her house is actually three small structures, one of which is the kitchen. She belongs to the Wuduke band society and is not a member of any Christian denomination.

Living with her is her daughter, in her early twenties, and the daughter's lover, about twenty-eight. This man is from an interior Grebo *dako* and is self-employed as a tailor, working out of their home. The daughter is a marketeer in Harper, holds natal citizenship in Wuduke through her father, and attends a Pentecostal church in New Kru Town. Her lover is not a member of any church or society.

To supplement her income, the household head takes in a family of renters, including a twenty-year-old student, his lover, and their child. The young man is from an interior *dako* as is his lover, who is a marketeer in Harper. They have a two-year-old daughter, who was born in Harper City.

Female-Headed, Civilized. The female head of this household, a sixty-year-old widow, is a very prominent and widely respected figure in the civilized community as well as belonging to the *pano* that holds the *wodo baa* position in Gbenelu. She was born in Ghana of immigrant Glebo parents, was married briefly and separated, but had her three children by another Glebo man who was not her legal husband. She still uses the title "Mistress" and the name of her legal husband, however. She has a wage job as a "matron" in one of the local high schools and is provided with a small apartment on the school campus. Her own house in Hoffman Station is run in her absence by her youngest daughter. This woman is a pillar of the St. James church and is considered to be a "town woman" or female elder of Hoffman Station.

In the apartment on the school campus, the female head is raising three granddaughters, aged fifteen, nine, and three, who are the children of her oldest daughter, living elsewhere in Liberia. She also has with her a nephew (brother's son), age twelve, and an eleven-year-old boy who is a servant. All the children except the youngest attend school.

At the house in Hoffman Station, where the female head lives when school is not in session, is the youngest daughter, age twenty-six, her three children (aged eight, two, and one), and her servant, an eleven-year-old boy whose mother is her friend. A sixteen-year-old girl who is the head's niece (brother's daughter) and a severely handicapped deaf man in his forties, the head's cousin (father's brother's son), also reside here. The resident daughter has another child, a five-year-old girl, who lives with a female relative of her father in a nearby house. She visits her mother frequently and is provided with clothing and school uniforms by her mother's family. All of the household members attend the St. James church.

From the above examples, it may be seen that these households differ both in their need for and ability to attract labor. Of the two native households, one is a nuclear family engaged in farming. The woman, who is the main subsistence provider, is able to feed her family without the assistance of others. She has, in addition, little but strenuous farm labor in an area isolated from towns and schools to offer potential recruits to her household. Probably her only source of help with her work is to convince her husband to marry another wife or wait until her children are older. The native woman in Wuduke, however, has no husband for whom she must farm and

[105]

can concentrate her efforts on marketing. She is in a better position to attract household help, both through her daughter and as a property owner in a desirable rental area. She was therefore able to retire from full-time marketing, although she keeps her small table set up at home to provide extra cash. These examples also demonstrate the wide variation in household organization and recruitment which exist within the native category. Although both farmers and marketeers are alike in their lack of formal education and in their ties to the native Glebo community, their economic strategies and domestic arrangements are strikingly different. In the following chapter, the connections between household composition and occupation for native women will be explored in more detail.

The two civilized households, both male- and female-headed, offer training and education to the numerous children they are raising as well as prestige and connections to locally prominent families. Both the male and female heads of these civilized households have achieved high status in the community by virtue of their age; they are both "fully grown" and responsible for large numbers of dependents. They have also demonstrated their commitment to civilized institutions such as the church and the educational system and belong to local *pane* with which they maintain close ties; they are not strangers in Hoffman Station, but "owners of the land."

Common to both the civilized households and the female-headed native household is the presence of dependent, adult daughters, some with children of their own. Such daughters are typical of the younger generation of civilized women who have been unsuccessful in establishing formal marriages. Unless they can find a job in the wage sector, they are dependent for support on their natal families and on gifts from men with whom they are currently involved or from former lovers who have fathered their children. Young women often make strategic decisions when considering a new relationship, testing the man's generosity both to themselves and to their household and researching his willingness to support his offspring by other women. A reasonably dependable man with a steady job will usually be welcomed into the daughter's (or foster daughter's) household, presented with food, and accorded sleeping privileges. His already having several such "wives" does not seem to inhibit the formation of a new relationship. Most civilized and native households seem to view their adolescent and young adult females as an important means of recruiting additional labor and resources, an attitude which is similar to that documented for the Kpelle by Bledsoe (1980).

The important exception to this easy acceptance of daughters' lovers is the case of civilized schoolgirls because a large investment depends on their ability to avoid pregnancy. Once a girl has "spoiled herself" by becoming pregnant before she has acquired enough education to get a wage job, however, her lover's position vis-à-vis her household changes from one of threat to that of potential contributor. Young men often find themselves the object of continuous, competing demands from a number of households and affiliated kin groups. Although they may complain bitterly, they continue to enjoy the peer-group prestige that accrues from having fathered many children by different women. Children of such unions who are acknowledged by their fathers (and most, for reasons of prestige, are acknowledged gladly) belong, patrilineally, to his *dako* and *pano* and may be claimed at any time after infancy. Although fathers have the right, ultimately, to decide where their children will reside, most stay with their mothers and are raised in the households of their maternal grandparents. This living arrangement is an important mechanism of household recruitment, and there are few older people who have not been "given" a grandchild or two to assist them around the house. Children are also routinely sent to be raised by their grandparents in the relative rural safety of Cape Palmas by sons and daughters living in Monrovia.

Native households that are not involved in subsistence agriculture, especially households headed by professional market women, often recruit household members in a similar fashion. Among native Glebo households that depend on rice farming, patterns of betrothal, bridewealth exchange, and patrilocal residence mean that household recruitment takes place through the incorporation of sons' wives rather than daughters' husbands. Also, in most farming families, a son who has married is likely to set up a household independent of his parents, although within the same *pano* and probably near his father's house. Although daughters' husbands may have certain ritual and customary obligations to their in-laws, they are not viewed as potential sources of household support as they are in the nonagricultural communities.

Although civilized women desperately need extra labor in their households to avoid doing work that would define them as native, they also have something very concrete to offer in return: civilization itself. Because of the flow of related and unrelated children and young people into civilized homes, these households tend to be larger than those of native agriculturists. The average number of persons per household is nine in Hoffman Station as opposed to five in Gbenelu. The configuration of the household and the presence of servants and foster children would therefore appear to be an accurate measure of that domestic unit's status, but there is an important exception to this general rule. As mentioned above, the households of professional market women more resemble those of civilized women than of the female farmers with whom market women share native status. Market women have similar demands for additional domestic labor so they can coordinate their business activities with their duties in the home. They are also year-round residents of the Harper area and have ready access to cash. Like civilized women, they can offer room and board to students in return for cash or labor and are committed to educating and civilizing their own children. Market women, therefore, share similar domestic arrangements and aspirations with civilized women but cannot hope to attain civilized status for themselves. Just as the labeling of a diverse, multiethnic community like Wuduke as "native" masks the complexity that exists on the level of individual practice, so the native status of market women would seem to mask similar complexity.

[5]

Economic Options and
Women's Independence

Certain economic options, namely, farming and marketing, define a woman's status as native rather than civilized. Native women, permanently prohibited from raising their status, might be expected to feel some ambivalence about a prestige system that assigns them the lowest place (i.e., native and female). Some female farmers work hard to plant and sell extra market crops to provide tuition for their children, fostered in civilized homes, but others have little interest in or inclination toward civilized life. Many native women consider themselves the proud bearers of Glebo tradition, deriving pleasure and a positive sense of self from the roles their culture provides. Other native women are year-round residents of the city or the civilized towns, speak fluent Liberian English, and have civilized husbands, lovers, and children. Their orientations to the complex of values associated with civilization are obviously different from those of the first group.

There are also significant economic differences between these two categories of native women. Women's economic independence is a practical manifestation of the native Glebo gender construction of woman as provider. In this sense, market women and female farmers are equally native because both retain the primary responsibility for feeding their families. This point has frequently been missed by other analysts, who view women's marketing as supplementary to the household income provided by a wage-earning man (Handwerker 1974, 1979; Hasselman 1979). I will argue that the earnings of market women, rather than those of their husbands and

[109]

lovers, provide the daily sustenance for their households, just as the rice produced by the farm woman feeds her family every day. Market women, however, fulfill this responsibility through an alternate economic strategy, which gives them a different relationship to the processes by which a person becomes civilized.

The civilized woman, by contrast, is not expected to be the primary economic support of her household; this responsibility is to be taken over by a man. What can she do, however, if there is no man willing or able to take on this role in her household? Civilized women have developed their own set of strategies in an effort both to retain high status and to achieve economic self-sufficiency. Taken together, these strategies resemble those of secluded Islamic women such as the Hausa of northern Nigeria. Specifically, civilized women depend on the labor of children, and their large, complex households are organized to this end. There are, therefore, three basic economic strategies Glebo women may pursue outside of the wage sector, depending on their status: farming, public marketing, and what I have called the alternate marketing system.

Subsistence Farming

As I have not worked extensively with female subsistence farmers, the following analysis is based primarily on published sources as well as on some limited observations on upland rice farms and discussions with informants. The major point, however, which will also be stressed in the following sections, is the centrality of women's responsibility for feeding their families.

A recent U.S. AID project, "A Profile of Liberian Women in Development," sums up women's crucial productive role: "The rice which sustains life for most Liberians and the cultivation of which forms the base of the Liberian economy is primarily produced and allocated by Liberian women. Their critical role in rice production underlies the operation of the customary legal system under which the majority of Liberian women continue to live. The necessity of learning how to cultivate rice is a key constraint in the attendance of girls in the formal education system" (Carter and Mends-Cole 1982:1).

The implications of women's subsistence contribution for other aspects of their lives are especially clear among peoples like the Glebo in southeastern Liberia, where rice production is almost exclusively a female activity and males provide much less labor than elsewhere in the country. Throughout Liberia, however, "men are dependent upon women for the production of the rice they consume. A man cannot make a rice farm without a wife, but a woman can make a rice farm without a husband" (ibid.:37).

The rice-producing cycle begins in January for Glebo female farmers, when the site for the year's farm is selected and "brushed" or cleared. The farm must be on land which is recognized as belonging to the farmer's town of natal citizenship or that of her husband. Although land disputes between the Glebo towns are frequent, they have not yet begun to experience the shortages felt by northern *dakwe*, whose farmland has been taken for concession agriculture. Farmlands are typically a day's walk or more from the coastal towns and usually five to twenty minutes from the farm village, the small house or cluster of houses occupied by a single household during the farming season. Men are supposed to be responsible for felling the largest trees, but women wielding axes have been known to clear their own sites without assistance. Either before or after brushing, when the contours of the land can be seen more clearly, the site is divided into separate plots, one for each adult woman in the household. From this time on, the women work individually on their own sections, and the rice produced by each is under her exclusive control. This pattern differs from that of northwestern Liberia, where all the adult women of the household farm one large plot under the direction of the head wife, who also controls the allocation of the crop. Since each woman is responsible for feeding her own children and husband from her individual field in the southeast, there are none of the personal farms planted by women for their private use and/or sale, as have been documented for other areas (ibid:70, 62; Currens 1976:361–62).

After brushing, the cut bush must be allowed to dry so that it will burn easily and deposit an even layer of fertilizing ash over the field. Burning usually takes place in the Glebo area in March, followed by the clearing away of unburned material and the planting, usually in April. Although achieving a "good burn" is the primary male contribution to farming, women have been known to assist and even take over this task in the absence of male help. Planting and weeding are exclusively women's work, and "bird scaring," which must be done to protect the ripening crop for several weeks before the harvest begins, is carried out primarily by children armed with stones and slingshots. Jeanette Carter and Joyce Mends-Cole have noted that the increasing enrollment of children in school conflicts with the need for child labor at crucial points in the rice cycle (1982:74–75).

Harvesting takes place from late July through October, with different varieties of rice ripening at different rates. Men may assist in the harvest, particularly if there is some urgency such as the fear of early rain, but this, again, is women's work. Co-wives who have labored individually on their separate plots may band together at this point, harvesting each woman's crop in turn until all the rice is in.

By mid-November, most Glebo have returned to their coastal towns for several months of holidays, incorporating Christmas, New Year's Day, and the birthday of former President W. V. S. Tubman (a national holiday). Elaborate funeral dances for those who died during the past year are held at this time, and everyone rejoices in the new rice and comparative leisure. By mid-January, the coastal towns are once again deserted as the people move back to the interior to begin new farms.

Although rice is the staple and most important crop in the female farmer's inventory, every woman grows a small vegetable garden for home consumption, a plot of cassava to carry the family through periods when the rice is running short, and extra root and vegetable crops to sell for cash. While women are occupied with farming, men may hunt, build fences around the fields to keep out pests, collect forest products like palm nuts and palm wine, or devote their time to cash crops such as rubber and sugarcane. As one woman put it, they also spend many hours sitting in the shade, "talking the things of the town" such as politics and witchcraft cases.

Because they are responsible for the rice, women generally do not have time for extensive cash cropping on the side. Their market crops are the same ones they grow for their own family's consumption, and only the surplus, if there is one, is sold. Vegetables like eggplant, bitterball, okra, and pepper are planted among the rice, and cassava is grown in the abandoned rice field of the year before. Cassava gardens are also planted close to the habitation site and on the poor soils of the savanna immediately behind the coastal towns. A woman will thus find a crop of cassava tubers, planted as budding sticks in December, awaiting her arrival on the coast the following November.

Both G. E. Currens (1976) and Carter and Mends-Cole (1982) note that the demands of the subsistence crop limit the amount of labor time available for cash crop production. "Cash cropping has been integrated into, not substituted for, the traditional subsistence production system. There has been an implicit compartmentalization of agricultural activities. The growing of upland rice on the annual household farm has not yet been touched by commercializing influences" (Currens 1976:364).

With the rice crop occupying most of their time and energy, Glebo women have not been able to increase their profits by experimenting with cash crops. The sexual division of labor leaves much more free time to men, allowing them comparatively greater access to cash-generating activities. A woman's ability to provide for herself and her children also leaves men free for long- or short-term labor migration, both within Liberia and abroad (Moran 1986). Farming, in other words, makes a woman independent of male labor but places her at a disadvantage in obtaining the consumer items needed by farm families: clothing, cooking equipment and other tools, seasonings, matches, and soap, among others. To get the cash for these items, as well as for a variety of social and ritual requirements, the farmer must depend on her husband's willingness to provide her with cash or she must market at least part of her crop. Since she usually does not have time to sit, day after day, in the Harper General Market, she depends on a professional marketeer to give her a good wholesale price.

Marketing

The surplus vegetable and tuber crops produced by female farmers are rarely marketed directly to consumers. Rather, a group of middle women or professional marketeers stands between agri-

[113]

culturalists and the non-food-producing population on the coast. This group performs an intermediary role between native farmers and civilized housewives. All three categories of women meet and interact, both economically and socially, at the daily market in Harper.

The Harper General Market is a large, roofed, open-sided structure, built by President Tubman in the 1960s. Although the interior is equipped with twenty-eight raised stone counters, each shared by two sellers, this space is inadequate for the number of marketeers who come to sell every day; as a result, the market building is surrounded on three sides by additional tables and stalls. Inside, counters for the sale of fresh meat and fish were included in the original design, but the sinks and fluorescent lighting are no longer operational (Figure 18).

It often seems that more actual commerce takes place outside of the market structure than within it, on the steps, along the alleyways on either side, and on the muddy bank of the river immediately behind the building. Whether they have one of the permanent counters inside, a roofed stall built onto the side of the building, a simple table of their own, or merely sit on a low bench beside a pan of farina (toasted cassava meal), all sellers in the market must pay a monthly fee of one dollar and fifty cents and a daily fee of five cents to government collectors. The market is open six days a week, from sunrise to sunset. Ultimately under the jurisdiction of the mayor of Harper City, its day-to-day operation is supervised by a market women's "chief," elected by the women themselves. Representing the city and county government is a male market supervisor, who oversees the fish, meat, and dry-goods trade which is the preserve of men. The Fanti community, which provides most of the fish sold in the market, also has its male representative, who is recognized by the government. The number of trading "firms" (Handwerker 1979:367), including fishing crews and permanent Mandingo-owned shops, is probably close to three hundred. Roughly two hundred of these firms are individual women traders who work full time at their businesses, conduct their own wholesale buying, bulking, bulk-breaking, and retailing, and live and support others on the profits of their enterprises.

The map of the Harper General Market is keyed to an inventory

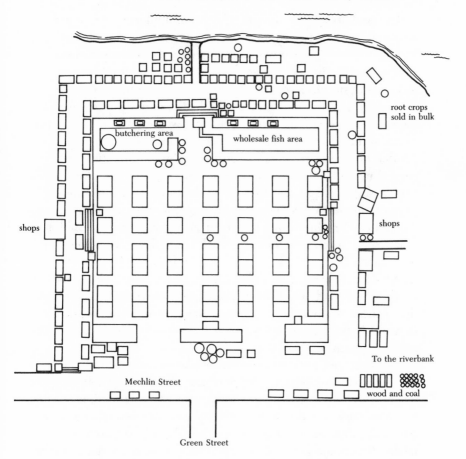

Figure 18. Harper General Market, redrawn by Imogene Lim from an original by Sao Varmah (not to scale).

which I conducted on February 7 and 8, 1983. In addition, I conducted interviews with sixty Kru and Grebo-speaking market women between June 28 and July 13 of that same year. Of the roughly two hundred full-time female traders in the Harper market, about sixty are indigenous to southeastern Liberia, with Mandingo and Fula women (who specialize in pepper imported from Guinea) and Fanti women (who specialize in fish) excluded. Both of these latter groups are recognized as foreigners by Liberian citizens and to-

[115]

gether probably make up half (about one hundred) of the women who sell every day. The sample of women was not chosen randomly. Rather, I began with a core group of women who were my closest friends in the market and at whose tables I was always welcome to sit, observe, and assist with selling. I then moved out to women in neighboring stalls until I had apparently exhausted the population of Kru- and Grebo-speaking women.

The interior and surrounding space of the market is functionally divided into "departments" according to the commodities sold. The central market house is primarily devoted to the sale of imported (American) rice, salt, tomato paste, bouillon cubes, dried and fresh pepper, onions, and a few other, mostly imported, condiments and medicines. Freshly butchered beef and goat meat are sold sporadically from the counter at the back left of the market house, and fresh fish is both wholesaled and retailed from the back right counter by Fanti fishermen, who bring their large oceangoing canoes up to the riverbank behind the market. In times when fish are scarce, the entire catch may be sold before it is even brought off the boats to women standing knee deep in water, shouting their offers as the crews come in to shore.

The left rear area outside the market structure and the area around the steps leading down to the alley on the left side are where most of this fish, fresh, dried, smoked, and salted, is retailed to consumers (see Illustration 4). Immediately behind the market structure is the area dominated by the sale of fresh produce, vegetables, fruits, and palm oil. To the right rear is an open area on the riverbank where cassava, eddoes, yams, and palm nuts are brought by farmers, spread on the ground, and sold in lots. Most of these are quickly bought up by the professional marketeers, who sell them on the stalls and tables in smaller lots more convenient to the daily shopper. In the alley on the right side of the market building is found a mixed assortment of rice, produce, snacks like fried cassava and plantain, and the stalls of male Mandingo traders selling imported dry goods, used clothing, and cosmetics. The front right corner of the market house is the preserve of Mandingo women, who sell dried pepper, kola nuts, and peanuts; market women of other ethnic groups who also deal in pepper get their stocks from the Mandingoes. On the street immediately fronting the market,

Illustration 4. Native market women selling dried and smoked fish on the side steps of the Harper General Market, 1983.

children set up small stands to sell snacks such as cookies, popcorn, candy, frozen soft drinks, and chilled drinking water. Mechlin Street, where it reaches the riverbank just past the market, becomes a dirt road and provides an area for the sale of firewood, sacks of charcoal, and chickens, goats, and pigs when they are available. Although most of these distinct departments overlap considerably and an anomalous table shows up here or there, a woman's location in the market is a rough indicator of the commodities in which she is dealing at that time.

Market Survey Results

Of the sixty women in my survey, 42 percent (twenty-five) were Glebo, 47 percent (twenty-eight) were Grebo-speakers from other interior or coastal *dakwe*, 10 percent (six) identified themselves as Kru, and 2 percent (one) as Krahn. Forty-eight, or 80 percent of the women, had had no formal education and were illiterate, 13 percent (eight) had attended school for one to five years, and 7 percent (four) claimed more than five years in school. The highest level of education attained was the fourth grade. This lack of formal education is consistent with the findings of Al-Hassan Conteh et al., who report that 81 percent of Monrovia market women have never been to school (1982:27).

The Harper market women were, for the most part, born and raised in Maryland County, 37 percent (twenty-two) in Cape Palmas (including the coastal Glebo towns), 47 percent (twenty-eight) in the interior or on the Garroway coast, and 10 percent (six) on the Kru coast. Only 3 percent (two) were born in Monrovia and 3 percent (two) abroad, in both cases in Ghana. The marketeers tend to live within the city of Harper, and few have more than a fifteen-minute walk to and from the market each day. Sixty percent (thirty-six) live in Harper itself, 27 percent (sixteen) in Hoffman Station, 7 percent (four) in Waa Hodo Wodo, 3 percent (two) in Wuduke, and 3 percent (two) in Gbenelu. Karl H. Hasselman, in his Gbarnga research, found it "very surprising" that 96 percent of his sample lived in the town itself with only 4 percent coming in from the surrounding villages (1979:194). Since 32 percent of the women in Hasselman's survey came from households that were primarily engaged in farming, he expected them to live farther from town. Residence close to the market site, however, is consistent with a shift to full-time marketing from the periodic selling of surplus crops by a subsistence farmer. Of the two women in my sample who were living in the native town Gbenelu, one was young and unmarried, living with her parents and putting her market earnings primarily into clothes for herself. The other was an impoverished widow who sold *fufu*, a kind of dough made from pounded, fermented cassava, which she grew and processed herself. Neither of these women was typical of the professional marketeer in Harper. It would seem, therefore, that a change in residence from the native towns to civilized towns or city neighborhoods accompanies a woman's shift to full-time marketing. Keeping in mind that most adult female farmers spend very little time actually living in the native towns, it would seem that women who wish to move into marketing are removing themselves from the authority of their natal and marital *pane* and from the labor demands of farm households. This hypothesis is supported by the high proportion of these women who claim to be independent heads of their own households.

The marital status of the Harper market women is presented in Table 10, compared with the results of a U.S. AID study on marketing that sampled 146 women in twenty-six markets all over Liberia (Kaba et al. 1982).

A noticeable difference between the two sets of data is the smaller percentage of Harper women who report themselves to be married. Even if we add the 8 percent who are in a "loving" or secondary wife relationship with a nonresident "husband," the figure still seems low when compared with that from the larger sample. Conteh et al. found that 78 percent of their sample of Monrovia marketeers were married (1982:29), and Hasselman's study of marketing in Gbarnga, the capital of Bong County in western Liberia, seems to indicate that 100 percent of the sixty-nine women interviewed had "husbands" (1979:196–97).

Of all the available studies of marketing in Liberia, Hasselman's work in Gbarnga is probably most comparable to the situation in Harper. Gbarnga, like Harper, is a county capital and a regional marketing center for surrounding agricultural producers, yet on a scale smaller than that of Monrovia. The number of women who trade there daily (about 230) is also comparable to that of the Harper market. There are, however, some interesting variations, as demonstrated in Table 11.

Table 10. Marital status of market women

Marital status	Harper		National study*
Married	59%	(35)	81%
Divorced/separated	10%	(6)	4%
Widowed	8%	(5)	8.2%
Single/never married	15%	(9)	6.8%
"Loving"/secondary wife	8%	(5)	0

*From Kaba et al. 1982:A-1 (real numbers not available).

[119]

Table 11. Household size of market women

Harper			Gbarnga*	
Number in household	Percent		Number in household	Percent
Self alone	3%	(2)	Self alone	0
2–5	30%	(18)	2–5	2%
6–8	23%	(14)	6–8	10%
9–13	32%	(19)	9–13	62%
14+	12%	(7)	14+	26%

*From Hasselman 1979:195 (real numbers not available).

Hasselman found that each market woman in Gbarnga was living with an average of 9.5 other persons (1979:195). The women in my survey of Harper seemed to be more evenly distributed among households of various sizes, although the greatest percentage lived in households of between 9 and 13 persons. It will be remembered from Chapter 4 that the civilized households of Hoffman Station averaged about 9 persons as compared with the smaller farming households of Gbenelu, which contained an average of 5 persons. Market women frequently mentioned the presence of relatives, foster children, and servants in their households, and in this way they resemble the complex extended families of civilized women.

Another difference between Hasselman's findings and my own is the number of persons contributing to the support of these households. The large Gbarnga households contained other wage earners or subsistence producers; in not one of the households in Hasselman's survey did the market woman provide the only income. In contrast, 27 percent (sixteen) of the women in my sample reported that their market earnings were the sole support of themselves and others, usually children, foster children, and relatives. Forty-seven percent (twenty-eight) reported that their husbands were working; 18 percent (eleven) were married to men who were unemployed. Thirty-three percent (twenty) had no husbands (the total of Divorced/separated, Widowed, and Single/never married categories in Table 10). Brahima D. Kaba et al. emphasize that many of the women in their study were married to men who were either unemployed or in relatively low-paying and unreliable jobs (1982:33).

Hasselman, on the other hand, found that 68 percent of market women's husbands in his sample were cash crop farmers, 19 percent were in market-related jobs such as drivers, butchers, and traders, and the remainder were retired or unwilling to give any information (1979:197).

In terms of commodity specialization, 28 percent (seventeen) of the Harper women sold fresh produce; 23 percent (fourteen), imported rice, dried pepper, and farina; 28 percent (seventeen), imported seasonings, country medicine (herbs and other medicinal and cosmetic preparations), and Western medicines such as aspirin, chloroquin (for malaria), and antibiotics (which may be purchased without a prescription in Liberia). Twelve percent (seven) of the women sold fresh or dried fish; 3 percent (two), processed palm oil; 2 percent (one), *fufu;* and 3 percent (two) specialized in snacks such as fried fish, cassava, and plantain. My sample does not reflect the commodity distribution of the market as a whole because groups such as the Mandingoes and the Fanti, who deal in specialized products, were excluded. The sale of freshly butchered meat is controlled by men, who both deal in livestock and work as butchers.

Although 27 percent (sixteen) of the women regularly travel to up-country markets in the interior, usually held on Saturdays, to buy their commodities, the majority either buy imported goods locally from Lebanese stores (37 percent) or let the country people come to them (17 percent). Although the goods, particularly agricultural products, can be obtained more cheaply in the interior, the added cost of carfare and transportation fees as well as a one- or two-day absence from the market make traveling to obtain goods less attractive than one might expect. Transportation costs for most locally grown foodstuffs are borne primarily by the producers themselves; female farmers must hire a transport car to get themselves and their goods to market. Much produce is also head-loaded from the interior to the coast by women and children on periodic visits to town during the farming season. Women who deal in dried pepper buy in the market from Mandingo women, who seem to have a monopoly on this product. Fish sellers (12 percent) buy from local Fanti fishermen. A very small percentage (2 to 3 percent) buy primarily in Monrovia or regional centers like Pleebo. Fully 82

[121]

percent of the women report that they buy their stock with cash; another 10 percent routinely buy with credit, and 7 percent use both methods from time to time.

Estimates of the amount of capital required to start in the market ranged from under three dollars (15 percent) to two hundred dollars and over (7 percent); most, however, started with relatively modest sums of between five and twenty-five dollars (43 percent). Although 38 percent (twenty-three) received their initial working capital from husbands or boyfriends, this figure is low compared with the national study conducted by Kaba et al., which found that 63 percent of the women began business in this way. Seventeen percent of the women in my sample received their initial capital from parents or other relatives, 5 percent from grown children, 10 percent with credit, and 30 percent claimed they used "my own self money" to get started in business.

To some extent, commodity specialization is indicative of economic stratification among market women. Forty-two percent of the Harper women claimed that their daily earnings amounted to between one and three dollars. Twelve percent reported making between ten and fifteen dollars a day, while 38 percent brought home between four and nine dollars. Only one reported her daily income to be over fifteen dollars. It is uncertain how reliable this information is, given the unwillingness to discuss income and the different ways in which the women keep track of profits and losses. Many keep the sales proceeds from each commodity separate and do not total their earnings at the end of the day. Kaba et al. report in their national study: "Information gathered from group discussions indicate that professional market women make very little profit from their marketing activities. As a result, very little capital formation occurs in this sector of the marketing system. As already pointed out, the main motivation for getting involved in marketing for the majority of sellers was not the profit motive but rather the necessity of taking care wholly or partly of essential household requirements such as food expenses, payment of children's school fees, clothing, etc." (1982:68).

Data from the national report yielded estimates of between $1,000 and $3,000 worth of yearly marketing capital for the average professional market woman, with profit ranges of from 5 to 25 percent or a net profit of $50 to $750 a year (ibid.:77). Hasselman estimated the monthly net profit of Gbarnga market women at roughly $43 a month, noting that such an income is comparable with that earned by a storeboy, unskilled worker, houseboy, or postman (1979:201, 203). The margin of profit a woman can make, however, is largely dependent on the commodities sold, which is a function of the amount of investment capital with which a woman enters business.

A common way of getting into marketing is to buy (or credit) a hundred-pound sack of imported American rice, which sells in Harper for $28.50. The rice is then sold by the individual "cup," a standard-size plastic drinking tumbler, to consumers who cannot afford a whole bag but need enough for their daily meals. The price of rice, however, is strictly regulated by the government; the price of a cup was set in 1983 at thirty cents and the penalties for over-charging include impoundment of goods, a fine, or both. The wom-en know that each sack of rice contains approximately 113 cups and that the first 95 cups sold represent only the return of the initial investment ($28.50). The remaining 18 or so cups, at thirty cents each, are the profit, or about $5.40, a fairly low rate of return considering the hours put in, the effort of hauling hundred-pound sacks about, and so on. A number of market sellers told me that they had begun by selling rice but that because "there was no money in it," they moved into other commodities. For many, how-ever, getting together even the $28.50 needed to begin may be very difficult and, given the low level of capital formation noted by Kaba et al. and the quick dispersal of profits into household mainte-nance, most women remain at this minimal rate of return.

Food items such as rice, however, are in constant demand, which guarantees that some small profit will be made each day to keep food on the market woman's own table. For those who have operat-ing capital beyond what is needed to secure a daily living from the sale of foodstuffs, however, there are additional commodities that yield a higher rate of return. Thirty dollars' worth of antibiotic capsules, sold slowly over a period of several months at fifteen cents each, can return one hundred dollars, clear profit, according to one informant. It is from the sale of drugs, cosmetics, and other nonfood items that this woman as been able to support three children through the University of Liberia and others through high school. Of the salt fish, sesame seed, and other food items which she sells, she says, "they are just for eating," that is, for everyday household expenses. The women who deal in Western medicines, indigenous herbal remedies, and nonstaple food products turn the largest profits and also require the most start-up capital, up to two hundred dollars to "open the table." It is therefore not surprising that two of the most successful traders in these items were once the country wives of two members of a wealthy and powerful repatriate family and were started in business by their husbands.

A wealthy sponsor can help a woman get started in the more lucrative commodities, but what happens to her business after that is generally up to her. Although the majority (68 percent) of the sample reported that their market earnings went to "eating," providing food for their families in accordance with traditional constructions of women's responsibilities, others mentioned school fees for children (8 percent), emergency medical treatment (2 percent), and personal items such as clothing (5 percent) as the ways they spent their profits. Often, there is literally no take-home pay in the form of cash because market women do their own marketing as goods come in and purchase their household supplies from their earnings, sending the food home to be cooked and eaten. Although the women with husbands for the most part expected their spouses to provide school fees for children, most also said that "the woman must help" with this family expense. Sixty-nine percent of the sample had between one and six children in school and 15 percent had seven or more for whom tuition, fees, uniforms, books, and supplies had to be provided. In the openended portion of the interview, women often expressed satisfaction at being able to "help my children and myself" and emphasized their contributions to the home even when the husband was relatively well employed. One woman became almost indignant when asked if any of her husband's wages went toward food, saying, "I will not waste my husband's money." "Market women, therefore, hold a strong position within the productive society and they are economically equal to certain male groups. They contribute efficiently to the support of the household often in the same way as the husband, the brother, and the son" (Hasselman 1979:203).

[124]

But to achieve this level of economic parity, and sometimes just to survive, the Harper market women must put in long hours in the market while still carrying out their domestic duties in the home, the proverbial "double day" faced by working women everywhere. Seventy percent of the women in Hasselman's Gbarnga survey spent ten to twelve hours a day in the market, six and sometimes seven days a week. The minimum workday was found to be six hours (ibid.:197–98). Conteh et al. refer to "market time" as a different chronological system than standard Western business hours, a literally endless cycle of buying and selling for some Monrovia marketeers, who even sleep in their market stalls (1982:21).

In addition to providing the food for their families, full-time market women are primarily responsible for cooking, an often arduous and time-consuming process under local conditions. So they can devote business hours to the market, this responsibility must be delegated to someone else, usually children and adolescents. Fifty percent of my sample receive help from their children in the market itself, carrying loads, running errands, and minding the table in their mother's absence. Some children take over the market tables in the afternoon after school, while their mothers go home to cook the family meal. Most women in my survey, however, rely on children at home to do the cooking as well. Only 28 percent of the total sample report that they must cook for their households in addition to their market business. The responsibility for seeing that cooking and other chores are done, however, lies with the female head of the house no matter who actually does the work.

Women can combine marketing and child care by keeping young children with them in the market, where they play and often sleep under the tables. Conteh et al. recognize the presence of large numbers of small children in the Monrovia markets as a "problem" and suggest that government-run day care centers might be a solution if women are willing to pay for them (1982:24). Kaba et al., however, found in their national survey that 74 percent of market women received no help with their market activities from children, a figure that seems unreasonably high (1982:77). Husbands were never mentioned as a source of help, either in the market or at home, in my survey or in any of the others.

[125]

Historically, Liberia has a very shallow marketing tradition. According to W. Penn Handwerker, "Unlike elsewhere in West Africa, in Liberia trade in marketplaces has become commonplace only within the last 2 decades, perhaps especially within the last 10 years." Indeed, only 22 percent (thirteen) of the Harper women had been engaged in marketing for fifteen years or more, and 18 percent (eleven) had begun during the previous year. The majority, 27 percent (sixteen), had between six and ten years of experience in the market. Few, however, were carrying on a family tradition in marketing; only 15 percent said they had learned marketing skills from their mothers, foster mothers, or older female relatives. Eighty percent of my sample claimed to have learned through trial and error and by watching others. These findings are consistent with Handwerker's data from Monrovia (1974:231, 236).

Looking to the future, though many women are assisted by their daughters, foster daughters, and younger female relatives, their ambitions for these young people do not include the market. The great majority of these daughters are already attending school; as they get older, they will be less and less willing to be seen sitting behind a market table. Several women told me that their daughters used to help them but now are "too big" (in their middle and late teens) and so stay home to cook. In the national survey, 90 percent of the women said that they wanted all their children, girls and boys, to attend school. When asked if they wanted their daughters to be traders like themselves, only 14 percent said yes and 86 percent preferred that their daughters become "office women and teachers," in other words, "civilized women" (Kaba et al. 1982:77, A-3).

The desire of West African market women to prepare their daughters for wage work as opposed to independent business was noted by Sidney Mintz in an article discussing the unintended consequences of this choice: "And schooling (for one's female children, at least), long the best way to raise the status of one's offspring to a point higher than one's own, seems directed mainly toward moving those children into occupations (such as nurse, teacher, welfare worker) long regarded in western society as the most obvious non-manual, low-status slots for women. Perhaps we are entitled to ask ourselves whether this sort of westernization . . . will not eventuate in lower status for women than was true traditionally, rather than a higher status, in at least some regards" (1971:253).

Mintz's question brings us back to the issue of each woman's motivation for going into full-time marketing, the other options she perceives, and the relative status between market women, female farmers, and civilized women. Kaba et al. attribute the movement of women into marketing to male labor migration and the resulting shortage of agricultural labor: "The drastic dwindling of needed male labor in the domestic and subsistence agricultural sectors may be construed as one of the most important factors of women's labor shift from the agricultural sector to the service sector of marketing" (1982:14).

Handwerker (1973, 1974) supports this formulation, arguing that women enter marketing largely as a result of the uncertainty of male wages and the failure of men to provide adequately for the family's support. Technological change and the introduction of a money economy, according to Handwerker, brought about changes such that "not only was there created a differentiated set of niches in which people could subsist without having to produce their own food, there was created simultaneously a backwash of unskilled and illiterate men, women, and children who had no salable skills, or at least no skills assuring them of a reasonably permanent or well-paying attachment to these niches. The traders of the Liberian market system—indeed, traders in general—originated out of a context in which money came to be used to meet subsistence wants but in which there were few, if any, alternatives for earning money without the requisite skills" (1974:233).

Although it is certainly true that large numbers of unskilled (in Western economic terms) men have entered the nonagricultural work force in the last thirty years, I believe that both Handwerker and Kaba et al. begin their analyses with a fundamental misconception about the role of male contributions to domestic subsistence. In discussing the rural division of labor among the Bassa, Handwerker says: "Men were expected to be the main source of subsistence" (ibid.:237). I believe, for the Glebo and possibly for other Liberian peoples, that this is simply not true. Hasselman, who worked primarily with Kpelle and Mandingo women in Gbarnga, seems also to take this perspective: "For many women of the traditional agricultural society, marketing is an opportunity to substitute farming. Instead of being forced to cultivate enough acres to secure the food for children and husbands, women can produce the same value on the market" (1979:203).

Rather than taking over formerly male responsibilities, I believe that female participation in marketing is an alternate means of continuing to fulfill women's responsibilities in an urban or semiurban context. It is for this reason that market women, despite their facility with spoken English, business acumen, and occasional presence as a force on the local political scene, are still considered native women. The real difference between a civilized and a native woman is her overt role in providing the daily support of the household. Just as a female farmer does not need a husband to make a rice farm (Carter and Mends-Cole 1982:1), a market woman does not need a husband to make market. Women's economic autonomy, therefore, seems to be at the heart of the civilized/native dichotomy. The Harper market women clearly expressed delight in their independence: "I see, I want something, I don't go to anyone to give to me. I take my own self money and buy it." "I can enjoy the market. Get one dollar, turn it around to another dollar. Then, I eat. If you be in the house all day, you can't get nothing." And finally, a secondary wife, whose legally married co-wife also sells in the market, said, "If my husband sees money, he gives me a bag of rice. If not, the market feeds me."

Civilized Women and the Alternate Marketing System

The General Market in Harper is, without a doubt, the best place for a businesswoman to attract customers. For some, however, going into the market in any role but that of a consumer is not an option. Yet there are ways in which civilized women can participate indirectly in the retailing of snacks, handicrafts, and even agricultural produce. Most of the production and marketing of these items takes place in the home, similar to the "extra-market trade" of secluded Hausa women described by Polly Hill (1969:393). Having a small business does not, in and of itself, threaten a woman's status; on the contrary, she may be praised for helping her husband or natal household and for her thrift and enterprise. Both those with employed husbands and those without participate in this system; for some it is a major source of income while for others a small business provides money for extras and contributes toward a woman's sense of "helping my children."

There are numerous small businesses in which civilized women can engage. Most require at least a small amount of cash as capital or for equipment; some demand a more substantial investment. Popcorn, bought from the Lebanese stores, popped in a pot over the fire, and sold in small plastic bags for five cents each, is a popular product, especially since the only cash outlay is a few dollars for the popping corn and plastic bags. As with selling rice in the market, however, there is a very low margin of profit on this item. Bananas, mangoes, and coconuts, grown in the house yard, require no investment but are highly seasonal and generally available to everyone without paying for them. At one point during my stay, mangoes were so plentiful that they were selling for less than a penny each (e.g., six for five cents).

The more serious civilized businesswoman is usually involved in sewing, baking, or producing less commonly available snacks. Women who own large cast-iron dutch ovens that can be used on an open fire bake shortbread, biscuits, and cookies, which can be sold from a table by the front door or by children who walk about with trays on their heads. A woman fortunate enough to own or have access to a refrigerator will take advantage of the infrequent availability of electrical current to produce Kool-Aid, small plastic bags of frozen soft drink. Both baking and dealing in Kool-Aid involve the purchase of expensive ingredients like sugar, white flour, tinned margarine, baking powder, and drink mix. An insulated cooler is also needed to keep the Kool-Aid from melting before it can be sold. Both frozen snacks and baked goods find a ready market, however, and provide a fairly good rate of return. A woman's sales are maximized if she has children or foster children who can be sent out to well-traveled areas, particularly the local school yards, which sometimes resemble small markets with a high level of economic activity. In this way, civilized women can achieve a greater volume of sales than by simply selling to those who happen to pass by the door.

[129]

Although tailoring is almost exclusively a male occupation, some women own small foot- or hand-powered sewing machines and make extra money at dressmaking or sewing children's school uniforms. For a woman to be capable of making her own clothing and that of her children is a significant help to the household budget. The high cost of the machines, however, and the fact that sewing skills are jealously guarded by the men who make their livings as tailors, puts this option well beyond all but a few women.

Another option for a civilized woman is a cigarette table, a small, portable shop that can be set up at road intersections or wherever people congregate. The tables are built by local carpenters; they have a hinged top, which, when raised, can be leaned against a wall or help upright with strings tied to the lower section. The inside of both top and bottom sections are fitted with small shelves and racks like a miniature store, on which packages of cigarettes, matches, mosquito coils, hard candy, gum, and other snacks are displayed. Cigarettes are rarely sold a pack at a time; indeed, the seller may have only one or two packs as stock. Rather, they are sold individually for five or ten cents each, depending on the brand. Some proprietors buy loose tobacco and rolling papers to produce cheaper homemade cigarettes that sell at two for five cents. Other homemade snacks, like cookies or popcorn, may also be sold from the table.

Such a table might be set up by the front or back door, moved to a road intersection where people congregate in the evening (there to compete with other tables, mostly offering the same goods), and carried, on the head of a child, to events such as dances, funerals, parades, and so on. Few civilized women spend their evenings tending such tables at the crossroads; this would give the appearance of a market table and might reflect badly on the woman's reputation. Rather, a teenager or older child will be sent to sell if the owner of the table feels he or she can be trusted. The dependence on child labor has its drawbacks in such cases because children may be tempted to consume part of the stock, pressured to give treats to friends, or even cheated by an adult customer. Women complain constantly that their children "steal" from them; most freezers and cigarette tables are fitted with locks, and the keys are closely guarded. Cookies, loaves of bread, and frozen snacks are carefully counted and their exact cash value computed before the young sellers are sent out.

A woman with a small business of this type may find herself under pressure from friends or relatives to extend credit or even gifts from her limited stock. In contrast to professional market women, a civilized woman's trading activities are not, by definition, assumed to be her primary source of support. In actual fact, these small sidelines may contribute a major share of the household budget, especially for a woman with children who does not have a secure relationship with an employed man. One woman, in just such a position, found herself unable to restock her cigarette table after friends and neighbors took advantage of her good-natured approach to business. As she put it, "When you credit your friends, the table breaks down fast."

Finally, there are a few civilized women who deal in agricultural foodstuffs, although, again, in an indirect manner. One woman's husband has access to a small pickup truck through his job. Every Saturday the couple travels to a large regional market in the interior to buy not only the weekly supplies for the household (at prices cheaper than those in the Harper market) but also cassava, plantain, and palm oil expressly for sale. Back in Hoffman Station, the goods are divided into piles of three or four tubers or fruits each, just as in the market, then stacked on trays and head-loaded around town by the woman's sons and foster sons. The proceeds from this weekly trip provide most of the food budget for the household.

The almost covert nature of civilized women's economic activities warrants comparison with the situation among the Hausa. Although confined to their husbands' compounds for roughly "the first thirty-five years of their married lives" (Hill 1969:398), Hausa women enjoy considerable economic independence through the marketing of cooked food and craft items. Their seclusion and the Islamic injunction that men should support their wives release them from farm work, and the presence of co-wives, daughters-in-law, and sisters-in-law reduces the burden of housework and cooking on each woman. Traditions of fosterage assure that even a lone woman will be "given" a child until she has her own (see Smith 1981 for an extended discussion). Child labor is vital for purchasing materials, marketing the products, and maintaining women's extensive networks of information. Customers are generally young, unmarried men, schoolchildren, and secluded women in other compounds (Hill 1969:399; Remy 1975:364). Hausa women may also retail stocks of grain amassed by their husbands, sometimes for a commission or the right to add their own profit onto the husband's price. Hill has argued that, because of such opportunities, women are actively opposed to the establishment of new central markets, which would threaten their position as retailers (1969:396). It is somewhat ironic that unsecluded women among the Hausa (known as "free" women, a term synonymous with prostitute) have far fewer opportunities for acquiring wealth and the capital to invest in new ventures (Cohen 1969:64–65).

Clearly, civilized Glebo women do not operate under the same constraints as their Hausa counterparts. Yet there are interesting parallels. In both cases status and prestige considerations relegate women to privatized, nonvisible economic roles. In both cases, such roles are held to be highly desirable and are envied. Since poor rural Hausa women are not secluded and work as farm laborers, seclusion is associated both with the urban elite and with upward mobility. Dorothy Remy, who has worked with Hausa employees in a tobacco processing factory in Zaria, reports that men who migrate from the countryside to urban wage jobs aspire to earn enough to take fully secluded wives, even if this is not common in their villages (1975:363). The curtailing of civilized women's public economic activities (excluding white-collar or professional jobs) and the emphasis on male wages as the official source of household income are familiar here. Yet certain factors common to both the Nigerian and Liberian economies make it possible for small-scale, extramarket trading to provide women with some measure of autonomy.

According to my census figures, there are also some nineteen permanent home markets in Hoffman Station, three in Waa Hodo Wodo, and six in Wuduke; Gbenelu, Puduke, and Jeploke have none. These deal in common market products like rice, seasonings, and palm nuts. In general, prices are slightly higher at these home market tables than in the central market; they operate something like a convenience store for those not wishing to walk all the way into Harper. None of these are run by civilized women; once again, the stigma of the market precludes their doing so. Civilized women who get involved in limited marketing must, however, compete with home and full-time marketeers, who do not hesitate to take their wares into the market or the streets and who are less dependent upon the cooperation of children and teenagers. But in spite of the general lack of cash flow in the community as a whole, there seems to be enough business for everyone. Handwerker has shown that widespread economic instability actually generates a demand for large numbers of sellers in Monrovia. "In practice, uncertainties about minimizing marketing costs implied the importance of balanced, reciprocal, personal relationships with traders" (1979:374).

These personal relationships, known as "good customers," are important in obtaining credit in the face of unanticipated expenditures, as well as for the "dash," an extra handful of rice, tuber of cassava, or free cigarette added to the purchase of a friend or relative. The good customer relationship can be abused, as with the woman in the example cited above, which results in the failure either of the business or of the relationship. In either case, a two-way benefit is expected, and those not fulfilling their part of the bargain find their customers looking elsewhere: "In short, there was a substantial demand not for the services of supermarkets, but for cost-saving personal services. This implies low limits on the number of such ties any one trader could maintain. . . . Hence, there was a demand for large numbers of firms. . . . Even under the conditions of sharp price competition in Monrovia markets, the ratio of food-selling market sellers to households was exceptionally high; in 1970, for the sector of the population regularly purchasing at market places, this ratio was in the neighborhood of ten households per market seller" (ibid.:375).

This explanation helps us to understand why nearly every woman in Cape Palmas seems to be selling something, if only twenty-cent cakes of soap from a tray by the back door. It also highlights the intensely personal, social aspect of economic relations and points to the market as the locus of interaction between women of different status categories. Professional market women are good customers of specific female farmers, whose agricultural produce they buy on a regular basis. They in turn have good customers among the civilized women, who buy from them daily and to whom they are willing to extend credit from time to time. On the other hand, one of the many professional market women who reside in Hoffman Station might send her son next door every morning to buy bread from her civilized neighbor—good customers again.

In the status hierarchy that rigorously defines women as either native or civilized, there is no physical separation or ban on friendships, which cross status lines. Civilized women still speak Glebo as a first language and, as we have seen in the preceding chapter, the ideology of residential segregation does not exist in practice. Frequently women are tied together through the fostering relationship; a native agriculturalist whose son or daughter is being raised in a civilized home routinely sends rice and other supplies to the house. These contributions may be sold by the foster mother, but they are contributions nonetheless and form the basis of long-standing friendships between the respective women.

Although their economic independence marks them as inherently native, market women seem almost an intermediate category between civilized and native. They themselves often use the terms *native* and *country* to refer to agriculturalists, although they would not classify themselves as civilized. What is more, their belief in education for their children indicates a commitment to the status hierarchy as it exists and to moving their children up within its ranks. Their relatively secure economic status and urban location also make them sought after as foster mothers for the children of aspiring friends and relatives. Like civilized women, market women need the domestic labor of children to carry on their business activities. Although they may not be able to offer the full range of training provided in a civilized home, they do serve as an alternate route to education and upward mobility for less well-connected rural children. As Hasselman notes: "Market women act as a social 'in-between group.' In this case [Gbarnga], they are very closely connected to their rural families from whom they get the goods, but they reside in an 'urban milieu.' Therefore, they will be an important information channel, connecting the existing different rural and urban levels of social life, and they will be the persons receiving, accepting, or rejecting urban influences. Market women are socially influential when they give money to their husbands . . . or when they distribute money to other family members" (1979:203)

This "in-between group" goes formally unrecognized by the civilized/native prestige dichotomy the Glebo use to categorize persons, households, and towns. Yet market women can rise to prominence and the most influential are widely respected by civilized and native alike. The chief of the Harper Market Women's Association also sits on the Maryland County Citizen's Council, an appointed body that advises the superintendent on local affairs. Several Harper market women now in their forties and fifties were once the *lappa* wives of repatriate men holding high national and county positions in the previous government. Although their husbands are now dead and the children of those unions living abroad or in Monrovia, these women still command respect and even awe in Harper. All of these women used their personal relationships with powerful men to build diverse, well-financed businesses in the market and rely on these businesses now that their patrons are gone.

One might ask, then, what is the point of striving for civilized status when economic independence, a life free from agricultural toil, and a respectable social position are available to the uneducated woman with a good head for business? Clearly, the market women themselves see their situation as much less than idyllic, since they are making every effort to educate and civilize their daughters. At the same time, it almost appears as though market women are attempting to construct a third category within the civilized/native dichotomy, one that would acknowledge their importance to the urban economy and accord them a level of prestige intermediate between native and civilized. If such a category were incorporated into the Glebo scheme, perhaps market women would turn their energies to training their daughters in business skills rather than leaving them overeducated for the market and undereducated for the wage sector. The prestige system might stabilize with a three-part hierarchy, providing the possibility of upward mobility for native women past the age of training for civilization. But Glebo institutions rigidly enforce the two-category system. As will be seen in Chapter 6, even the Episcopal church sharply distinguishes between civilized and *lappa* women. The emphasis on clothing style as the ultimate marker of status and the explicit equation of "making market" with a woman's loss of prestige block any attempts by market women to claim even a modicum of civilization. Yet the market also serves as a safety net for civilized women with nowhere else to turn. Although she is transmuted from civilized to native by the market, a woman can use it as a short-term strategy to survive a particularly difficult period. A prominent civilized woman in Hoffman Station was planning to visit her foster daughter, whom she had raised and trained in her home. The foster daughter had married and moved to the Ivory Coast, but before the mother could make the trip, she learned that the young woman's husband had lost his job. Stranded in a foreign country, the foster daughter had put on *lappas* and taken up marketing to support them both. Fearing that a visit at such a time would "embarrass them both too much," the foster mother postponed the trip, saying that she would wait until the husband found work again and the daughter could "wear dresses."

The market women in my survey seemed to emphasize literacy and education as the key factors in determining their choice of occupation. When asked what other work they would like to do, the typical reply was, "What else can I do? I don't 'know book,' so I have to go in the market." In spite of the high numbers of unemployed civilized people around them, they still have faith in the ability of schooling to raise their children's status. At the moment, the Harper market women seem to view themselves in much the same way as Hasselman sees them—as a transitional generation, the last natives in their particular family lines. Whether this becomes true will depend on the ability of the Liberian economy to absorb their educated sons and daughters. If conditions remain as they are today, it is likely that at least some of these daughters will be forced to return to the marketing strategy they knew as children; of them it will be said, "They used to be civilized."

[6]

The Management of Status: Women and the Glebo Community

In the preceding chapters, I have discussed the separation of Glebo women into status categories which rank them, one over another. The categories may have appeared more divisive than they are in practice. Just as there is no real residential segregation of civilized and native Glebo, there is no social segregation either. Because of family choices regarding fosterage and the limited resources available for investment in education, many civilized women have full sisters who are rice farmers and mothers who sell in the market. Status considerations do not cut these women off from one another; rather, there exists an almost constant flow of goods and services in both directions. This chapter describes these reciprocal relationships and the associational memberships that extend them beyond the realm of kinship. The marshaling of resources which takes place following the death of a Glebo adult provides the context in which to view these reciprocal relationships, as family and association members strive to fulfill their obligations to the dead.

Types of Group and Organization Membership

We have seen that all Glebo hold ascribed membership in the *pano*, town, and *dako* of their fathers. Shared membership in any of these units may be a compelling reason for one individual to make a request or extend aid, usually financial, to another. Civilized people, presumed by natives always to have money, frequently complain about the endless demands of their "country people" for cash and gifts. Fraenkel likewise noted that the civilized Siklipo of Grand Cess found *panton* obligations falling most heavily on their shoulders (1966:168). My civilized informants, however, also complained about the stinginess of their native kin, wondering why they did not send more gifts of rice, cassava, and other foodstuffs from the farms to their suffering relatives in town. Fostered children who travel to their hometowns for school vacations always carry dried fish and baked products, gifts from their foster mothers, and return with bush meat, rice, and forest products for their host families. Native men and women in Harper on market or cash crop business can be sure of a meal and a place to sleep in the homes of civilized *pano*-mates, and civilized people making trips "home" to their ancestral towns expect equal hospitality.

Since most fostered children are related to the families with which they stay, such a relationship may be viewed as an extension of the reciprocal exchanges within the *pano*. The entire *pano*, including members living far from Cape Palmas, may be called upon in extraordinary circumstances, as when an important member dies, is jailed, or faces some other calamity. Networks of kin, affinal, and fictive kinship links (through fosterage) ramify widely for each individual and represent a sometimes dormant but easily revived system of support.

In addition to links through kinship and fosterage, Glebo of different status categories are joined through their common membership in Christian churches. The very early and lasting impact of Christian missionaries on the Cape Palmas Glebo and their coastal and interior neighbors was discussed in an earlier chapter. Table 12 illustrates the percentage of the Gbenelu cluster population over sixteen years of age that claims affiliation with a church or other religious organization. The figures are drawn from my census data and may reflect informants' equating church membership with the regular payment of dues and tithes. Therefore, although an unknown proportion of the "No church membership" group might attend services from time to time and consider themselves to be Christians, they do not claim to be church members. The distribution of church members across the six towns once again highlights the differences between native and civilized towns discussed in Chapter 4.

Table 12. Church membership for population age 16 and over

Town	Males				Females			
	No church membership		Church members		No church membership		Church members	
Hoffman Station	39%	(137)	61%	(211)	32%	(110)	68%	(233)
Wuduke	47%	(93)	53%	(105)	39%	(66)	61%	(104)
Jeploke	58%	(29)	42%	(21)	52%	(26)	48%	(24)
Waa Hodo Wodo	35%	(18)	65%	(34)	31%	(20)	69%	(44)
Gbenelu	68%	(43)	32%	(20)	78%	(51)	22%	(14)
Puduke	98%	(40)	2%	(1)	96%	(44)	4%	(2)

More men than women consider themselves to be church members in Gbenelu, while the opposite is true in Hoffman Station, Wuduke, Jeploke, and Waa Hodo Wodo. It is possible that since church affiliation is viewed as at least one aspect of being civilized and therefore of high status, native men are more likely to join as a result of their greater access to cash, facility with English, and generally more extensive knowledge of Western ways. This conclusion is borne out by the fact that many of these male church members are elders of the *takae,* that is, the heads of their local *pano* units. Many older Glebo men and women, with an eye to the future, seem to view the churches as just another form of the traditional band societies, which provide elaborate funerals for their members at death. Both the *wodo baa,* who is also the town chief of Gbenelu, and the paramount chief of the Nyomowe chiefdom are members in good standing of the St. James Church in Hoffman Station. Likewise, the clan chief, who is also the *wodo baa* of Puduke, is the only male citizen of that town who belongs to a church. Participation by the paramount, clan, and town chiefs in the church emphasizes their standing as the representatives of their people to the civilized, Christian, government of Liberia. The *bodio* and *gyide,* as well as certain other indigenous religious specialists may not enter a church building under any circumstances.

In the civilized community, it is not necessary to be a regular churchgoer or even a token member of a denomination to claim civilized status. In fact, people often state clearly that "civilization is different from Christianity" and point to the native portion of the congregation, attending services in *lappas,* as an illustration. Indeed, the St. James Church, which can legitimately be viewed as the spiritual and emotional center of the civilized Glebo community in Hoffman Station, recognizes and even regulates the status differences among its members, but significantly, only for women. The church's annual tithe is set by the resident Glebo priest and his governing committee at a rate of five dollars for men, three dollars for mission women (*mesa nyeno*), and two dollars for *lappa* women (*nyeno ko dado,* literally, women having cloth). This difference reflects the presumed differential access to cash of women in the two categories, while at the same time reinforcing and institutionalizing the status hierarchy.

Although the Episcopal mission has historically been the most active among the Glebo, it holds no monopoly on their loyalties. As illustrated in Table 13, the two Glebo churches, St. James in

Table 13. Religious affiliation of population age 16 and over

Religious affiliation	Hoffman Station	Wuduke	Jeploke	Waa Hodo Wodo	Gbenelu	Puduke
St. James	29%	17%	21%	7%	11%	1%
	204	62	21	8	14	1
Ascension	7%	5%	1%	12%	1%	0
	46	19	1	14	1	0
St. Marks	1%	.5%	0	0	0	0
	7	2				
Other Episcopal	1%	2%	1%	2%	0	0
	10	8	1	2		
Methodist	10%	5%	8%	4%	2%	0
	66	20	8	5	3	
Catholic	7%	4%	2%	3%	1%	0
	51	15	2	4	2	
Baptist	.5%	.5%	0	1%	0	0
	4	1		1		
Pentecostal	7%	20%	12%	35%	11%	2%
	46	74	12	41	14	2
Jehovah's Witnesses	1%	1%	0	3%	0	0
	8	5		3		
Islamic	.5%	1%	0	0	0	0
	2	3				
None	36%	44%	55%	33%	74%	97%
	247	159	55	38	94	84
Total	100%	100%	100%	100%	100%	100%
	691	368	100	116	128	87

Hoffman Station and Ascension across the river in Harper, attract the majority of churchgoers in the Gbenelu cluster. St. Mark's, located in the center of Harper and attracting a mostly repatriate congregation, and the other Episcopal churches at Spring Hill, East Harper, and the various coastal Glebo towns, also have their adherents.

The Methodist church, which concentrated its missionary activities on the Garroway area and the Kru Coast, is the next largest of the established denominations, followed by the Catholics (also influential among the Kru) and the Baptists. The fastest growing groups appear to be various Pentecostal churches; some, like the Assembly of God, have ties to missionary groups in the United States while others simply form around an individual claiming the power of prophecy and healing. The leaders of these independent or "Prophet" churches are often women, and their personal followings range from a few neighbors to large congregations with permanent church buildings. Pentecostal prayer meetings and healing sessions may be attended by members of other denominations; they are a popular form of entertainment as well as spiritual solace since their services consist primarily of dancing, drumming, singing, and inspired preaching. The Jehovah's Witnesses, who are often politically suspect because they refuse to salute the Liberian flag, attract only a tiny minority of the population, and the few Moslems are immigrant Mandingoes and Fullah traders from Guinea, temporarily residing in the community.

Although parents usually bring their children to the same church in which they hold membership, it is not uncommon to find a variety of religious affiliations within the same household. Of the three high schools serving the Cape Palmas region, two are church-affiliated (Episcopal and Catholic) and students attending them may be encouraged to participate in the sponsoring church. Likewise, many of the primary and junior high schools are operated by the churches. Different religious preferences are not seen as an impediment to marriage, and husbands and wives are likely to continue attending (and financially supporting) their chosen denominations. There is also some movement of individuals between churches; concern was raised in the St. James Church when the Pentecostal denomination in Wuduke began providing caskets, free of charge, for its members upon death. Such an attractive membership bonus was feared for the effect it might have on St. James's congregation.

The shifting nature of religious affiliation becomes clear when an individual dies without a clearly established relationship to a particular church. In one case that I followed closely, a civilized Glebo man, professionally employed as a medical technician and in his early forties, died suddenly at his home in Jeploke of unknown causes. Although he had been baptized and confirmed in the St. James church, he had allowed his membership (and the yearly payment of tithes) to lapse for some years. Shortly before his death, he had been attending services at a Pentecostal Prophet church in Harper, hoping for relief from a recurring medical problem. Upon his death, the local civilized branch of his *pano* turned to the Episcopal priest at St. James. The priest was the dead man's affine, married to his cousin (father's brother's daughter), yet because the deceased was several years behind on his yearly tithe, the priest could neither preside over the wake and funeral in his official capacity nor allow the body to be brought into the church before burial.

Concerned that some religious service was needed, the dead man's sister, a native woman, and her interior Grebo husband approached the Prophet church's pastor to ask if he would conduct the wake and funeral from his church in the New Kru Town section of Harper. The pastor replied that the deceased was not a member of his church either, that is, "his name was not in their book." The sister and her husband gave the pastor sixteen dollars to write her brother's name in the book, but this set off a conflict with the Episcopalian side of the family, who had arranged for a modified service at the deceased's home to be run by lay leaders from St. James. Eventually, the Prophet congregation arrived in force on the day the body was formally laid out, but only to "visit the family" and not to conduct the formal wake. The wake was performed by the St. James lay leaders; the priest attended, but as a member of the family and not in his vestments. Likewise, the funeral on the following day was held at the house and again with the lay leaders presiding, although the Prophet congregation was again present. Many of those attending commented about the funeral being held at home and not in the church and discussed the importance of keeping up with church dues because "you never know when death will come." The implication was that had the man known of his impending death, he would have taken steps to become clearly attached to one church or the other. Furthermore, by insisting on a service conducted through the Episcopal church, the dead man's civilized relatives made it clear that they, as civilized people, were better equipped to conduct a proper Christian wake and funeral than the native sister.

In addition to basic membership, the churches sponsor a number of men's, women's, and youth groups, prayer bands, junior and senior choirs, altar guilds, and so on. In any one congregation, the memberships of the various organizations tend to overlap to a considerable degree; thus I knew of several Hoffman Station individuals who, in addition to belonging to the St. James Church, held memberships in the Gospel Chorus, the Girls Friendly Society, the St. James Youth, the Regional Episcopal Youth League, and the Episcopal Church Women. In keeping with the Glebo definition of maturity, the youth organizations often include people in their thirties and forties. These groups perform services related to the care and upkeep of the church such as clearing the grass and bush growing around the building, sweeping and cleaning the interior, and caring for the graveyard located beside the church. The groups also offer programs or entertainment events featuring songs, skits, and recitations followed by a rally or request for the audience to come forward with donations. The queen rally, which seems to be a peculiarly Liberian institution, is something of a cross between a beauty contest and a celebrity telethon and is an especially popular way of making money. Disco dances are among the other events which church groups offer to the community, usually taking place in the church's school building. Funds are used to send delegates to regional and national meetings, to buy materials for distinctive hats or T-shirts for all the members, or to make a group donation to the church. Although, like the churches themselves, these church-based voluntary associations are open to anyone wishing to join, in practice most draw their membership from the civilized adult and student population.

On the "native side," there are other groups which restrict their membership to "country people." The most public of these are the band societies or *kumli* (a Glebo variant of the English word

[143]

company), whose activities are, like that of the churches, a central aspect of wakes and funerals. The societies are, in a sense, insurance organizations because the dues collected from each member through life are paid out to the family upon death. Rather than survivors' benefits, however, these funds are specifically to help defray the expenses of the funeral and, most important, to pay for the performance of a brass band in honor of the deceased.

I was unable to learn much about the origins of the Glebo brass bands except that they seem to exist in all of the major Glebo settlements and in some Nyabo towns as well. Presumably, the instruments and music were introduced by either the American colonists or the missionaries (probably the former), but the Glebo have embraced this Western musical form and made it their own. The instruments, many of which appear to be old, are highly prized and the periodic replacement of a few pieces is one of the most prestigious contributions of a paramount chief or other "big man" to his people. In one southern coastal Glebo town, when the citizens were asked by a United Nations Village Development team to list their "development priorities," they reportedly requested new band instruments as their most pressing need.

The music played by these bands consists of tunes similar to the polka in which a few phrases are repeated over and over. Instruments include the bass drum, trumpets, trombones, saxophones, French horns, and tubas, all of which are played by men. Bank performances are not limited to the activities of the societies but may be sponsored by anyone who can afford the payment of cash and liquor. Both civilized and native individuals may "call the band" to their houses to celebrate special occasions such as the birth of a long-awaited child or a high school graduation. At Christmas, New Year's Day, and on national holidays, the bands wander from house to house, playing for drinks and money.

Of the three *kumli* operating within the Gbenelu cluster (and which are said to belong to Wuduke, Jeploke, and Puduke, respectively), two own their own sets of instruments and have among their members men who know how to play them. The third society either contracts with one of the other two or hires an independent band, such as the Big Town Band of Gbenelu or the Cape Palmas Band, which seems to consist mainly of civilized men. However the

[144]

music is obtained, it is the duty of the society to provide a full night of dancing, from about 10 P.M. until dawn, while the body is laying in state, and to accompany the body to the grave with music. The society also provides money for the casket and helps the family with their obligations to distribute food and liquor to those attending the wake and funeral. The band societies are open to both men and women and, in the native towns at least, enjoy a very high rate of participation by the population over the age of sixteen.

The term *society* may be applied to other groups besides the *kumli*. Women, teenagers, and younger men and women may join singing and dancing groups known as *glorro*, a term that does not appear in Innes's dictionary and for which I was unable to obtain a derivation or even a translation more elaborate than club or cultural troupe. These performance groups appear to be similar to the Sabo *wainyo* or "Wire companies" as described by McEvoy (1971:174–79). For example, the groups are generally sponsored by a prominent wealthy man who is said to "have" the company. Most of the members are girls and young women, but Glebo men do participate as drummers and among the singers and dancers, unlike the Sabo version, which seems to be exclusively female. Different *glorro* groups are distinguished by wearing identical cloth *lappas* and T-shirts printed with the name of the group; male members have the chosen cloth made into shirts and caps. Similar to the brass bands, the *glorro* may be called to perform at the house of a chief or other important person on national holidays or the occasion of a visit by a government delegation. They must also be paid with liquor and cash, which is divided among the members. *Glorro* groups often perform at the conclusion of the three periods of funeral dancing known as the false burial, especially if the dead person was relatively young. These performances begin late, at about midnight, and continue until dawn.

The civilized counterparts of the *glorro*, or cultural troupes, likewise wear identical costumes and perform for special occasions or national holidays. All songs are sung in Glebo and are considered to be "traditional" Glebo music, although the songs themselves go in and out of fashion and are probably of recent origin. Civilized people speak of the cultural troupes as valuable for "making the children proud" of their Glebo heritage. Membership in both the

[145]

civilized and native versions of *glorro* is voluntary, although an initial cash outlay is required for the dancing costume, and there may be regular dues. Attachment to these groups is casual, and I knew of many young women who were former members but "got tired of it" and left. Both the Sabo and Glebo singing and dancing groups share many of the features of the Kru women's associations described by Fraenkel for Monrovia (1964:178–84), and George Buelow for Grand Cess (1980–81:27–31).

Among other organizations for young people are men's football clubs (soccer teams) and their female supporters, who, in addition to athletic contests, sponsor parades, queen rallies, and programs to raise funds for uniforms and equipment. Their members are usually drawn from the civilized community simply because most organized sports take place in school yards. Like the dancing groups, a football club usually requires a wealthy patron; when I returned from Monrovia with a soccer ball for the children in my neighborhood, they immediately formed themselves into a team, named in my honor.

Similar in drawing their membership from the civilized youth are the so-called development associations whose aim is to "bring improvements" to the ancestral towns, whether or not the actual members have ever resided there. The improvements generally consist of projects like community latrines, which may or may not be wanted by the intended recipients. These "progressive youth associations," as Fraenkel calls them (1964:184), are more common in the migrant communities of large cities like Monrovia or Freetown (see also Little 1966; Banton 1957), but they are also popular with the students and young employed people of Harper. The development associations also sponsor programs, queen rallies, and dances, at which the music is provided by a Glebo brass band. The Gbenelu Development Association of Monrovia once sent all the way to Cape Palmas for the Big Town Band to play for one of its functions in the city, paying all their expenses for the round trip.

Women participate, at least marginally and sometimes prominently, in all of the above organizations. In addition, the market women of Harper have their Market Women's Association, which includes Glebo, interior Grebo, Kru, Fanti, and Mandingo women.

[146]

The members meet once a month, paying a monthly dues of twenty-five cents, and contribute additional funds when a member dies or loses a close relative. The market women appear collectively in identical *lappa* suits, like a *glorro* society, on holidays or other special occasions. Their leader, a Glebo woman who lives in Hoffman Station, is known as the market chief and settles disputes, assigns selling space in the market hall, and represents the women to the city mayor and on the county superintendent's Citizens Council.

Membership in kin groups and voluntary associations cuts across the civilized/native dichotomy and unites women of different status categories. Civilized women often take the leadership roles in church-related organizations like the Episcopal Church Women. In organizations such as the cultural troupes, however, a native woman will be recruited to teach the girls the "right way" to dance. Tonkin has argued that terms like *native* and *civilized* (*kui* and *zo*) are "not really binary oppositions but identify different domains of knowledge, power, and expertise" (1981:322). Although there may be moments of conflict over which domain should be invoked in any particular circumstance, most events and activities are already categorized according to the civilized/native scheme. Thus in events surrounding the established churches and, especially, the Episcopal church, civilized people are expected to take the lead. The prosecution of witchcraft cases, however, is left to native specialists.

As we have seen, it is possible for a single individual to have close ties on both the civilized and native sides of the community. Since the full breadth of a person's kinship and associational network is most visible in the events surrounding his or her funeral, such occasions are often the scene of much negotiation between civilized and native concepts of what constitutes a proper wake and burial. For a band society member and town elder who is also a member of a Christian church and has many civilized *pano*-mates, the entire range of required rituals can occupy several days, preceded by weeks of preparation. The Glebo manage to accommodate participation by all or most of the deceased's personal network only by careful scheduling and an impressive cash outlay. Since women

[147]

play an intense and important role in all Glebo funerary practices, their management of status considerations in the context of mourning and loss is particularly instructive.

Women and Obligations to the Dead

The observations on which this section is based were made during about twenty wakes and funerals, uncounted visits to bereaved families, and two successive seasons of commemorative dancing for the dead. It has frequently been noted that women's role in the expression of grief and mourning and their responsibilities to the dead tend to be more elaborate than that of men (Danforth 1982:31). Under conditions in which life expectancy is short and child mortality very high, a Glebo woman can expect to spend a significant portion of her life in mourning for children, relatives, affines, and husbands. In native Glebo towns, where little ritual attention is given to marriages or other life-cycle events, funerals and the dancing that follows them constitute the major ceremonial events of the year. In the civilized towns, wakes and burials are managed by the various Christian denominations, and numerous Western features have been adopted and adapted by local practice. The most elaborate performances are in honor of individuals with affiliations on "both sides," that is, native church members who also belong to one of the band societies. In such cases, the full ritual panoply of both native and civilized practice are combined.

When a person dies in either the civilized or native towns, it falls to the women of the household to inform the neighborhood with a public display of grief. If the death takes place in town and the deceased is an older person, is a member of the *takae*, or holds a similarly prominent position in the traditional hierarchy, members of the family (local *pano* unit) must bring a bottle of cane liquor to the *bodio* and *gyide* to inform them of the death. Failure to postpone crying for the deceased until after this duty has been performed will result in a serious fine; since the *bodio* and *gyide* are not allowed to see or touch a dead body, they must be warned to avoid that particular *pano* until after the burial. Once this responsibility has been carried out, the women of the household in which the death has taken place leave the house, weeping, sobbing, and shrieking, to wander through all the five contiguous towns of the Gbenelu cluster, calling out their relationship to the deceased. One of the most common yet continuously heartrending sounds in the Glebo community is that of a woman crying *na yu, na yu* (my child, my child) during any hour of the day or night.

Women are sometimes prone to almost self-destructive behavior in the first moments following the death, throwing themselves violently on the ground, rolling in the dust or mud (depending on the season of the year), and kicking or striking at those who come to assist them. Women who recognize the distraught person as a member of their own, their maternal, or an affinal *pano* realize that they, too, are bereaved and rush out to join the crying in the street. Both mourners and sympathizers eventually end up back at the *dum kae*, mourning house, in the *pano* to which the deceased belonged. Other women not so immediately affected as well as distant relatives just receiving the news will arrive throughout the day to join the mourning women "on the mat" (*dum kor*, literally, mourning mat), sitting on mats on the floor, where they cry and comfort one another.

There are no significant differences in the expression of grief by civilized and native Glebo women. In such times, other status considerations are suspended and all are bound together by a shared sense of loss. Behavior which in other situations would be expected of civilized persons, such as sitting off the ground on a chair or bench, is interpreted very differently in the context of a sympathy call; not to sit on the floor and cry with the family women is evidence that the caller is not really sorry, but secretly happy, that the person has died. Since all deaths are ultimately traceable to the evil actions of other human beings, such behavior would be tantamount to an admission of witchcraft.

If the death occurs during the agricultural season while people are scattered on their farms, other *pano* members and townspeople are informed by the blowing of wooden trumpets (if the deceased was an adult male) or by messengers dispatched with the news. In the case of an adult, most townspeople will leave their farms and come to the coastal settlement for a few days of mourning, followed by the band society wake and burial. The full night and day of

[149]

dancing, usually performed for adults, may be put off until after the harvest, when many such "false burials" are held. Even if the death occurs during a relatively slack period in the agricultural cycle, the dancing may be postponed to give the family a chance to marshal its resources for this very costly event.

Once the death is generally known, friends and relatives gather in the *pano* to which the deceased belonged or, in the case of civilized towns, in the house of the closest family members. Many deaths now take place at the hospital in Harper; the high mortality rate reflects not only the inadequate facilities but the fact that the hospital is usually the last resort for those already dying and beyond help. In such cases, the body is kept at the hospital morgue while the family returns home to receive visitors and plan for the funeral.

In the *pano* the men gather in one room, usually the parlor or reception room, while the women congregate in the kitchen or, sometimes, in another house in the same *pano*. The male head of the household in which the death has occurred must provide liquor for the male visitors, especially the other adult males of the *pano*. The women seat themselves on mats on the floor, legs extended stiffly out in front and hands on their heads in the classic Glebo position of mourning. The crying rises and falls as each new female family member or sympathizer arrives, beginning to weep as she enters the house. Removing her shoes or sandals (if she has them), she sinks to the ground among her relatives, who, if they have previously stopped, will begin crying again to join her. Others, less closely related, will rub the heads and shoulders of the mourners, telling them, "don't cry," "sorry, sorry," and "never mind." As all available floor space fills up with seated women, the crying dies down to an occasional sob and quiet conversation begins. There are many plans to be made, many obligations to be fulfilled, of which the crying is only the first. All Glebo women, civilized and native, are required to cry for deceased members of their own and their husbands' *pano* and usually for their mothers' and fathers' mothers' *pane* as well. For their own *pano* members, native women may be "on the mat," that is, sitting in the bereaved household and receiving visitors, for several weeks both before and after the burial. They are "paid" for their crying with gifts of liquor, contributed by their male family members and by sympathizing friends. Although civilized women of the *pano* do not actually stay on the mat (*dum kor*) for the duration of the mourning period, they will visit daily for several hours and bring cooked food for the women until they return to their farms. Younger women with families to feed are the first to leave, but older female relatives of the deceased with fewer responsibilities may stay on the mat for up to a month or even more.

The men in the front room or veranda are also engaged in making plans. If the death was that of an infant or child, the body will be washed and dressed and the casket prepared almost immediately. If the family has an affiliation with a Christian denomination, the body may be briefly "churched," brought to the church for a few prayers and then buried in the church graveyard. Infants are buried without ceremony in cardboard cartons; if it was its mother's first child to die, great effort will be taken not to allow the mother to cry because this may bring harm to the other children she will bear. If the child was older ("walking and talking"), and the family is not Christian, the casket will be brought into the room of mourning women for a last look before it is carried off and buried in the town's cemetery by younger men of the family. Most attention will be centered on the room where the men are meeting; since childhood deaths are usually attributed to witchcraft emanating from within the *pano*, this gathering takes on the function of an inquest. The women also discuss the possible conflicts within the *pano*, which might have led to the death, and often comment bitterly on the inability of the men, who "talk and talk" yet cannot "put a stop" to the killing of their children. When a series of childhood deaths occurs within the same town, the result may be a *tapanu*, or assembly of all the citizens, followed by accusations, confessions, or even the infamous sassywood trial by ordeal.

Although all deaths are presumed ultimately to have been caused by "witch," the Glebo do recognize that some individuals simply die of old age. If the person is very old and has been sick for some time, plans for the funeral may have been made in advance, especially by the band society, which will have to come up with large amounts of cash fairly quickly. The most tragic deaths are held to be those of teenagers and young to middle-aged adults, between the ages of about fifteen to fifty, since they, unlike the very old or the very young, are always certainly the victims of witchcraft. Also, a death in this age group is likely to catch the family unprepared, and further tension is created by the speed with which funds and resources must be mobilized.

Among the decisions facing the family at this time is whether to have the body embalmed and, if so, for how long. It is an expensive proposition, but one that allows the various events preceding the burial to take place without unseemly haste. The basic price for a "two-days" embalming in 1983 was one hundred dollars. The expense is considered necessary, however, especially if the deceased had children or siblings living elsewhere in Liberia or in other West African countries. They must be notified and given the time to come for the funeral, if possible. This is the case typically in civilized families, several members of which are likely to be living and working in Monrovia. Embalming, therefore, becomes a necessity in the moist tropical climate; in one case, seventeen days elapsed between the death and burial of a civilized man in his forties to allow relatives from all over the country to arrive in Cape Palmas. Western methods of embalming have spread even to the more remote coastal towns, and there are a number of native Glebo men who practice this profession as a sideline to their agricultural activities. The average period of time between death and burial in the cases I observed was about one week.

During the week or so before burial, the native female *pano* members will be on the mat continuously, visited every day by their civilized female kin, who come to sit with them for an hour or so every morning and evening. The St. James church makes every effort to schedule its members' wakes on Saturday nights with the funeral on the next day, Sunday afternoon. The band society wake, therefore, is usually held on Friday night or on Saturday night following the church people's wake. Both occasions require a display of generosity by the bereaved family in providing cane liquor, bottled beer and soft drinks, and sometimes beef soup from a specially butchered cow, not only for the band but for the society membership and neighbors and friends as well.

If the church is to be involved in the wake and funeral, the church women or adult civilized women of the *pano* will "dress the room" where the body is to be laid out. The front room or veranda of the house is cleared of all furniture and decorations and is sometimes given a new coat of whitewash. The civilized women gather flowers and greenery from the bush with which to decorate the walls, and white lace curtains, donated by one of the few prominent women who own them, are hung on the windows and doors of the room. White is considered to represent the spirits and is worn by those who become "prophets" and form their own churches; this color symbolism also occurs in the false burial rituals. If the deceased was a woman, her most beautiful cloths, collected during her lifetime and representing her accumulated wealth, will be hung on the walls and draped over the chairs on which the coffin rests. Older women who spent part of their lives in Ghana and Nigeria often owned elaborate kente cloths, cut velvets, laces, and cloth-of-gold, all of which will later be divided among their daughters or other female kin.

The casket is then brought in and set up on two chairs in the center of the room. The male elders of the *pano* must enter the room first, lift the lid, and view the body, commenting on the quality of the casket, lining, the new clothes, the preservation of the body, and so on, before it is viewed by the general public. This is the "laying out," which begins a series of public events at which the corpse is the center of attention. All responsible adults in both native and civilized communities are obligated to make a brief appearance at the house, view the body, and extend sympathy to the family.

The band society wake, conceived of as "paying back" the deceased member for what he or she contributed during life, usually begins late in the evening on the day the body was laid out. Often, the band does not begin playing until after midnight, although a crowd gathers and drinking has been going on throughout the day. The music is performed in front of the house where the body is lying in state; the casket is open and the room is lighted as brightly as possible so those still arriving can "see the face." One family even went to the expense of renting a small gas-powered generator to provide electric light during one of the power outages which are so common in the Harper area. Dancing, mostly by individual women, takes place both outside in the front yard and indoors, circling the casket. There is some dancing by male-female couples, but most of the men give their attention to drinking. Chairs are set up in small groups for the more important town elders, society officers, and civilized guests, and liquor, beer, and soft drinks are served. As in most Glebo dancing, the participants follow each other, single file, in a long line that weaves in and out of the house, around the casket, and through the seated groups of dignitaries. As the evening progresses, the dance may become less organized and children and teenagers form their own lines on the outskirts of the pool of light. In spite of the presence of the body, the mood is joyous; women dress in their best cloths, and liquor flows freely. The music, dancing, and drinking end at about dawn.

The church wake, if there is one, takes place on the following evening. That day, the civilized women are busy preparing the refreshments to be served; biscuits and "tea" (actually coffee) are considered the only appropriate offerings and again represent a considerable cash outlay. The ingredients for the biscuits, including white flour, sugar, tinned shortening, baking powder, and dry milk, are all imported items, which must be purchased from the Lebanese shops in Harper; the instant coffee, milk, and sugar for the "tea" also have to be purchased. In addition, serving a large crowd requires plastic or styrofoam cups and paper napkins for wrapping the biscuits. In spite of the difficulty and expense of securing these items, biscuits and coffee are considered such an integral part of the wake, at least in the Glebo Episcopal churches, that they are served even in the more remote towns. Both the cash outlay and the preparation are the responsibility of civilized women (see Illustration 5).

When a death occurs, the civilized women of the family join together and pool their money to buy ingredients for the baking. If they have difficulty raising the required amount, they may petition the men to help them with a contribution. Besides the items to be purchased, a large load of wood, about equal to an average family's cooking fuel for two or three weeks, must be acquired to keep the six or seven cast-iron ovens hot for several hours. Usually the wood, in the form of cut and partially charred tree trunks, can be obtained from the abandoned rice farm of a native relative; the difficulty is in finding a way to transport it to the coast. The Episcopal priest at St. James, who has a pickup truck provided by the church, is often

Illustration 5. A young civilized woman baking biscuits in a cast iron oven, Hoffman Station, 1983. Biscuits and tea are considered essential for a proper wake.

[155]

asked to help transport wood for baking; the women will then only have to pay the cost of the gas. The priest's pickup is the object of many requests related to wakes and funerals, transporting everything from bodies, coffins, and mourners to cases of soft drinks and beer.

Civilized women say that native women "don't know how" to bake and so they must take the responsibility, even if the deceased is not a close relative. In such cases, the native female relatives will contribute the materials and wood, decreasing the financial burden. The next step is to recruit labor, not a difficult process because all civilized church women recognize an obligation to participate, and the gathering is a pleasant occasion. In addition to herself, each woman brings her daughters, foster daughters, and female servants to help with the work. Baking is done outdoors, at the house of a civilized woman who is either related to or very friendly with the bereaved family. The hard work of handling the hot ovens is mostly delegated to teenaged girls, while older women split, butter, and wrap the finished biscuits in paper napkins. Like others who participate in funeral-related events, the bakers must be "paid" for their work with soft drinks and liquor, provided by the family.

The church wake, as conducted by the St. James Episcopal Church, consists of opening prayers over the closed casket, followed by the singing of hymns for several hours. While the body continues to lie in state in the decorated front room, most of the singing takes place outside in the front yard, which has been roofed over with a temporary structure of poles and palm thatch or zinc sheets in case of rain. Benches and chairs, brought from the church and school, are arranged in rows under the shelter. The St. James choir, made up mostly of young children, leads the singing, and most of the songs are taken from the Episcopal hymnal and tend to be slow, sad, and in English. Occasionally, a song in Glebo is suggested to "give our native people chance." The non-Christian female relatives of the deceased continue on the mat during the wake, sitting and often sleeping on the floor of the other rooms and passageways of the house.

At about 11 P.M., the priest or lay leader who is directing the wake reopens the casket and announces, "time for tributes." At this time, family members, friends, and representatives of all the organizations with which the deceased was involved come forward to pay their last respects and lay a crepe paper wreath on the coffin. Church-related groups, co-workers, savings clubs, *glorro* societies, development associations, and many other organizations come forward to speak a few words and sing a hymn around the casket. For an older person, tributes are often made by groups in which their children and grandchildren hold membership; for example, one elderly women received tributes from three local football clubs to which her athletic grandsons belonged. This part of the wake is almost a recital of the variety and nature of the social ties created by an individual during his or her lifetime. Sometime after midnight, when all the tributes have been made, the casket is again closed and the "tea" and biscuits are served.

The formal involvement of the church in the wake ends at this time, but some people may stay up all night with the body, singing, clapping, and drumming on the benches. They are especially likely to do so if the deceased was a young man or woman with many friends, or if there is a large cohort of children and grandchildren. The language of the songs shifts entirely to Glebo, and the style becomes similar to the spiritual style of the songs sung in the Pentecostal churches. Those remaining often split into two teams and competitively try to drown each other out. The sponsoring family will serve hot sweet coffee and biscuits as long as supplies last.

The day following the wake, typically a Sunday, the church funeral is held in the afternoon after the regular Sunday service. If the deceased is an older native man, his *sidibo* agemates bring the casket out of the house, lay it on the ground, and speak to the body, reminding it of its deeds in life and rehearsing the obligations it can expect from the townspeople, most of which have now been fulfilled. Wooden horns are blown and iron war rattles shaken during the speeches; then the body is turned over to the representatives of the church who have come to collect it. The coffin is loaded onto a pickup truck and the *sidibo* accompany it for a short distance out of town, then turn back before reaching the church.

In the case of a society funeral, the brass band, playing a slow and steady beat, marches ahead of the truck bearing the body, followed by the society members. The male and female members march as

[157]

separate companies, men in dark Western-style suits and women in black *lappas*, white blouses, and their brown velvet sashes. At the head of the society march two men carrying long wooden poles, each topped with a carved five-pointed star, and a third man with a ceremonial sword. At each intersection in the road on the way to the church, the men with the poles form an arch by holding the tops of the poles together; the entire company then marches through under the crossed stars. These maneuvers are "society business" for which no explanation or interpretation was offered. It is clear, however, that some elements, such as sashes, swords, and the five-pointed star symbol, have been borrowed from the Masonic lodges and other fraternal societies of the Harper repatriate community. Behind the truck with the body come the bereaved family and the other mourners lined up in rows about three abreast.

At the church, the body is received by the priest and his acolytes, who are waiting outside. The tolling of the church bell informs the community that the deceased was a "member in good standing" and as such is welcomed into the church for the last time. If the deceased was a woman, the Episcopal Church Women will wear their uniforms, consisting of white dresses and navy blue collars with "E.C.W." embroidered on them, and will sit together in a special section of the church. Members of the band society are likewise given a specific area in which to sit, as is the bereaved family. Special dignitaries, such as the paramount chief and town chiefs or representatives of the central government like the mayor of Harper, are seated in the front row of pews. A member of the family will be asked to read a life sketch, and the priest's sermon is likely to focus on the life of the dead as an example for the living. Particularly at the funeral of an older person, the priest will address the younger survivors, admonishing them to settle their own disputes and be kind to one another, now that their elder relative is no longer there to judge their cases and advise them.

When the service is ended and the body is about to be taken from the church, crying begins again among the female relatives and friends of the deceased. The sound of weeping, moaning, and shrieking reaches a climax as the body is loaded onto the bed of the pickup truck once more. Then the band strikes up and the mourners and the society regroup for the final procession. Since most church graveyards are located next to the church, the procession usually proceeds down the road a bit, circling around and doubling back on itself until it ends up back where it started, at the grave.

After the burial, the mourners return to the house where all the previous activities have taken place. There, the older native female relatives, who have remained on the mat and not attended the service at the church, are still crying and must be comforted. The band continues to play for a few hours, and more liquor and food, rice with beef soup, is served. The topic of conversation will likely be the last major decision facing the bereaved family: when to hold the false burial, or commemorative dancing, for their departed relative.

If the deceased was not a Christian, the false burial and the actual internment may coincide. The false burial consists of one night and a full day of dancing the *doklo*, "men's war dance," if the deceased was male and the *nana*, "women's war dance," if female. The *doklo* and *nana* are danced by, respectively, men and women, although persons of the opposite sex may join in at the end of the dance line "for fun." Participation is mandatory for all married or engaged women and men; refusal to dance is punished with a fine. Both *doklo* and *nana* are for "big people," that is, "fully grown" adults over fifty years of age at the time of the death. For younger adults, there is the *boya*, which is danced for the death of a woman of childbearing age, and the *kobo ta woda*, formerly associated with the return of men from labor migration overseas. Both the latter two dances are now rarely seen because families find themselves financially unable to bury their younger members properly. I was fortunate in being able to observe two performances of the *boya* during my stay, but to my knowledge, the *kobo ta woda* has not been danced for several years, and some say that its particular drum rhythm has been forgotten.

The timing of the false burial depends upon the point in the agricultural cycle at which the death occurs and the ability of the family once again to provide liquor for the entire town as well as visitors. In most cases, it is postponed to give the family time to prepare and "look for the money." Among the places where they will "look" are the homes of their civilized kin.

In November, when native Glebo return to the coastal towns

[159]

with the new rice harvest, there is usually a backlog of false burials waiting to be performed. The family may take several years to "make their false burial"; some never manage to accumulate the necessary resources, and though this is regretted, there are no sanctions or fines imposed in the face of obvious economic hardship. But in spite of the expense, the period from mid-November to late December is almost wholly taken up with false burials. The thirteen Glebo coastal towns often try to stagger their funeral dancing during this time to allow *pano* members from different towns the opportunity to meet all of their *pano* obligations during the season of false burials.

Civilized men, especially if they were politically prominent, also receive a false burial, sponsored by their native relatives. In such cases, it is appropriate for the civilized men of the community to dress as warriors in masks and animal skins and dance the "war dance" with the native men. I have observed high school principals and county government officials in full-dress battle attire, dancing ecstatically with cutlass in hand. I never witnessed a false burial for a civilized woman and I unfortunately never thought to ask if the *nana* was performed in such a case. At the false burials of several native women who were also church members, I was told that it was all right for civilized women to join in the dancing, "since she was a Christian." Indeed, I and my civilized friends danced at several *nana* and *boya*, but not in the appropriate woman's dance costume of two *lappas* worn without a blouse. The organization of the false burial is entirely in the hands of the native branch of the family, its proper enactment falling within their field of expertise. Tasks of serving drinks and candy, however, may be delegated to young civilized women of the family, under the direction of their native relatives. All civilized members of the *pano* are expected to make material contributions, either in cash or in goods, particularly of liquor. I once met a very prominent civilized man in Harper, complaining loudly as he purchased the four cases of beer his native *pano* members in Puduke had requested as his contribution to a *nana* they were sponsoring for one of his uncle's wives. His public laments at the manner in which "my country people are killing me" drew attention both to his stature in the community and to his financial ability to meet their request. At all these events a special section is reserved for seating civilized members of the family and their financial assistance is expected in return. Although the civilized people may refer to the false burials as "country custom," they acknowledge the strength of *pano* obligations (and the possibility of witchcraft as a sanction if these are not met) by the financial support of its activities (see also Fraenkel 1966).

Case Studies: The Management of Status

Times of grief, mourning, and tragedy draw Glebo women of different status categories together; throughout the various events surrounding an individual's death, they both affirm and deny the hierarchy that separates them. As has been pointed out, sympathy calls and a genuine display of emotion are enforced both through gossip and overt accusations of witchcraft. All women in the towns of the Gbenelu cluster recognize that death may strike in any family and at any time; the support of many, both in meeting financial and labor obligations and in providing emotional comfort and solidarity, will be needed someday. The common experience of losing a child, or a number of children, resonates through each woman's experience, native or civilized, and though the men may "talk it and talk it," looking for the witch, it is the women who hold each other, rub each other's heads, and mingle their tears.

Other relationships besides kinship are called into play which cut across status considerations. When an old woman from Jeploke died in 1983, her daughter and granddaughter, both professional marketeers, mobilized a wide network to meet their financial obligations. The Market Women's Association took up a contribution to help defray expenses, and many market women attended both the wake and the funeral. Various lines of credit with Lebanese merchants in Harper, forged through business relationships, were used to obtain the baking materials and drinks on easy terms. A particularly strong friendship, based on a good customer relationship, between the granddaughter and a prominent civilized woman, led to that woman taking charge of the church wake. She mobilized the Episcopal Church Women's organization to "dress the room" where the body was laid out and donated her own white lace cur-

[161]

tains to the effort. The biscuit baking was held at her house, again with labor recruited through the church organization. Since the dead woman's *pano* of marriage did not have a strong presence in the civilized community and her own civilized relations were financially strapped by another recent death, this aid by the granddaughter's friend was crucial in carrying off a proper church wake for the old woman. In this case, practices usually associated with kinship were explained in terms of a relationship from a different context (the market), and the women's friendship seemed unaffected by their asymmetrical statuses. Yet the status differences were made explicit when it was explained to me that the native women "don't know how" to make the proper preparations for a church wake. When the body was first laid out, the civilized friend disapproved of the dress the body was wearing, claiming that the lace was not fine enough for burial clothing. The clothing was later changed.

Finally, civilized women, like civilized men, often find themselves in the roles not only of consultants on how to run a proper wake, but of financial patrons to their native kin, being pressed for contributions they can barely afford. Yet a proper and dignified funeral is so highly valued that these responsibilities are not taken lightly. The following example demonstrates how a group of women banded together to give an elderly woman a modest funeral which her kin group could not afford.

The dead woman was a member of *gideklabo pano* and a natal citizen of the Kuniwe town of Waa who had spent most of her life, like many of her generation, in Ghana. She had married there but never had any children, considered a terrible fate for a Glebo woman. When her husband died and she returned to Cape Palmas as an old woman, she found she had little family left; various members of *gideklabo pano* (and its sections, *kla yuabo* and *nyema hnebo*) allowed her to stay with them for a few months at a time. At the time of her death, she was staying in Hoffman Station with an elderly civilized man who was the recognized head of the entire *pano* by virtue of his age. One day while returning from buying fish at the Fanti settlement, she stopped to rest at the home of a well-known civilized widow who was the leader of the St. James church prayer band and a "big woman" in church affairs. The widow's own mother had been a member of *gideklabo pano* (*nyema hnebo* section), and the old woman used to call her "my child." While resting there, the old woman died suddenly, leaving the serious problem of who was responsible for burying her.

Both the civilized widow and the elderly civilized man were taken by surprise, but they agreed that because the old woman had no local *pano* of marriage and no children, he, as the head of her natal *pano,* must arrange for the wake and funeral. The old man, however, was supporting a large household on a small government pension and had been impoverished by five family deaths within that same year; there were no resources left. The dead woman was decidedly native and since her arrival from Ghana had been attending the Pentecostal church in Wuduke but had not paid membership dues. Aside from that rather tenuous affiliation, she had few other ties in Cape Palmas.

The family men came to the conclusion that there was no money for embalming and not even enough for a coffin; the woman would have to be buried immediately without wake-keeping. The elderly *pano* head's two wives, finding such a decision intolerable, pooled their market earnings and bought a few rough wooden planks and a bottle of cane liquor, which they brought to a local carpenter and asked him to make a coffin; it was to be a simple box because the body was not to be laid out for viewing at a wake. But the civilized widow at whose house the death had occurred was also feeling her matrilateral responsibility. She went to a man belonging to a section of her late husband's *pano* in Gbenelu who practiced embalming and arranged to have the body embalmed for two days, the minimum amount of time, on credit. She confided to me that the cost was one hundred dollars, but that when she went to pay her affine, she would give him seventy dollars and he would accept it, in memory of her late husband, his relative.

The body preserved, a wake was then arranged in the Pentecostal church, which agreed to conduct the services "for charity." Those attending were primarily from St. James, there in honor of the prayer band leader. The Pentecostal church choir arrived late because most of its members were young women attending night school, but they kept a vigil over the body most of the night. Perhaps since it was held in the church rather than in a private

[163]

home, but more likely reflecting the scarcity of resources, there was no baking and no serving of biscuits or tea.

The next day, the funeral was held at the Pentecostal church and was well attended by *pano* members who had never met the deceased but who had been informed that their relative had died. The Episcopal priest from St. James assisted his Pentecostal colleague in the service, and the body was buried in the St. James cemetery. The mourners then returned to the house of the *gideklabo pano* head, who managed to come up with a large bottle of cane liquor to serve them. The conversation there centered on the various responsibilities of the family members and how well they had been met. The civilized widow, the elderly *pano* head, and his marketeer wives were all praised for "taking care of the family," and everyone agreed that they had done the best they could under the circumstances. The family was particularly grateful to their matrilateral relative, the civilized widow, who had made the wake-keeping possible. It was agreed that an immediate burial would not have been respectful of the deceased nor would it have reflected well on the family, but they had felt they had no other choice. It was the women of the family who had most deeply felt the impropriety of a hurried burial and who had made the personal sacrifices to meet their obligations to a long-lost relative.

The two cases presented above demonstrate both the collective efforts of native and civilized Glebo women in fulfilling their obligations to the dead and the separate duties their status positions define. In both cases, the wakes and funerals required the cooperation of native and civilized women in order to be judged appropriate by Glebo standards. Mutual dependence and exchanges of resources, labor, and expertise link women in a common effort, not masking or denying the status differences between them but constructing these as reciprocal. The daily crying of native female kin is as much an obligation, and a contribution, as the baking of biscuits for the church wake by the civilized women of the family.

Although status differences between women are dissolved in the first emotional outbreaks immediately following the death, they are soon reasserted as the family and associations begin to mobilize for the funeral. The funeral rituals do not seem to constitute a liminal period during which status considerations are suspended for either women or men (Turner 1969), and the civilized/native dichotomy becomes the organizing scheme behind the division of labor among women who have roles to play in the wake and funeral. Whereas civilized men meet their obligations simply by sending cash or a crate of beer, civilized women are more deeply involved in visiting, crying, making preparations, cooking, and other activities that demand both their labor and their time. Civilized women often find themselves allied with native women against their male relatives of both status categories as they argue for a better casket, more elaborate burial clothes, or some other expense which they feel the deceased is due. Women complain that men are more interested in buying the liquor, which they themselves will consume, to the point that they would be willing to send the dead "naked into the ground." Women view their organizational skills, knowledge of correct procedures, and guardianship of tradition as important resources which men should not challenge. The assignment of civilized and native labels to each in the series of rituals surrounding death, and the fact that any individual has multiple ties with both sides, allows women to pool their knowledge and skills in a joint effort.

[7]

Conclusions: Gender
and Prestige

African studies have provided fertile ground for the examination of social ranking and prestige management, both within and outside of formal political hierarchies (among others, Fortes and Evans-Pritchard 1962; Vincent 1968; Cohen 1981). West Africa in particular has also been the focus of unusual attention regarding the political and economic position of women in its indigenous societies (Little 1973; Paulme 1963; Green 1947; Leith-Ross 1939; Ottenberg 1959; Hafkin and Bay 1976; and others). One result of this research has been the recognition that many African political structures are gender-sensitive or dual-sex in nature (Lebeuf 1963; Okonjo 1976). The political organization of these societies acknowledges the division of the population by gender in the existence of parallel (although not necessarily homologous) sets of prestigious positions with political functions, one for women, the other for men. Men and women, therefore, neither represent each other in the public arena nor compete against each other for recognized and legitimate statuses (Moran 1989). Many of the famous West African women's protests of the colonial period have been reinterpreted as a response to the imposition of male-staffed courts and administrative hierarchies which consolidated legitimate power on only the men's side of the parallel structure (Ardener 1975; Van Allen 1972, 1976; Moran 1989). The indigenous Glebo status system is of the dual-sex type, upheld by the cultural construction of the genders as two separate, noncomplementary kinds of human beings. Increasing age grants prestige to both men and women, and sets of parallel positions, such as *wodo baa* and *blo nyene,* provide an opportunity for native women to rise within a hierarchy that is not dominated by men. Likewise, native women's control over basic agricultural resources provides them with a source of economic power and independence under the traditional system. In the civilized world, prestige and status, to say nothing of economic and political power, have come to be dependent upon the ability to work within the single-sex political systems modeled on the West. Men and women, armed with the knowledge acquired through a Western-style education, find themselves pitted against one another in a unitary system of ranking.

This is not to say that single-sex systems are not subject to subtle and not-so-subtle distinctions on the basis of gender, but rather that gender-sensitive positions within the hierarchy tend to be conceptualized as complementary rather than parallel. By complementary, I mean that the necessary tasks accompanying a particular status are divided between two individuals, only one of whom actually holds legitimate title to the position. This is not the same as saying that two statuses, such as husband and wife, are complementary to each other, but rather that a status like "elected official" includes duties carried out by another person besides the official himself. Thus, although the Glebo dual-sex system recognizes a town chief and a town women's chief, each independently elected and having no kinship or marital relationship to each other, the overarching Liberian single-sex administrative system supports only one set of offices, always filled by men, who are expected to represent both the male and female populations of the town. For a woman to participate in this system, she must either take on the role of a man and perform according to male standards (Okonjo 1976:45) or fulfill the complementary role expected of the wife of a male officeholder, entertaining guests and presiding at functions but without a legitimate status of her own. Of course, she may gain prestige from such activities, but this is derivative and dependent upon the continuation of her husband or other male relative in a particular status category. As was demonstrated above, the availability of a separate set of statuses and the opportunity to acquire prestige independently of a man becomes increasingly difficult when a woman is committed to a Westernized, civilized lifestyle.

[167]

At the same time, a commitment to a Westernized lifestyle becomes necessary in order to work within and through the structures of the current nation-state of Liberia.

The indigenous Glebo political system contrasts vividly with Ortner and Whitehead's argument that the public domain, dominated by men, is that in which "larger prestige structures take their shape. Simply put, the other-than-gender prestige hierarchies of most societies are, by and large, male games" (1981:18–19). Such a formulation seems to ignore the possibility of just such dual-sex hierarchies as I have been discussing. Furthermore, the assignment of "larger-than-gender" types of prestige to the so-called public domain would presumably banish gender to the private domain, ignoring the fact that gender operates in all aspects of social life, not just within the domestic unit. The assumption that societies can be divided into separate spheres labeled public and private has been extensively questioned (Bourque and Warren 1981; Rosaldo 1980), but more important in this case, precludes an understanding of what happens when women have no other than "male games" to play. In other words, when dual-sex systems are replaced or overlaid by single-sex ones, as has been a frequent result of colonialism, the new prestige hierarchy consists of only a single set of positions for which women and men must compete.

The concept of civilization, as introduced to the Glebo by traders, settlers, and missionaries, initially appears to be an example of a single-sex system of ranking, a unitary standard which both men and women can attain. Thus, though only a man might aspire to be *wodo ba* or a woman the *blo nyene*, both could aspire to civilization and attain it through the same route of formal education and training. But because single-sex systems are also patriarchal, "women can achieve distinction and recognition only by taking on the roles of men in public life and performing them well" (Okonjo 1976:45). I believe this is what Ortner and Whitehead have in mind when they speak of "male games." To perform well as a civilized person, a woman, as we have seen, must have either a well-paying professional job or maintain a binding relationship with a man who has one. The organization of the Liberian state is such that considerably more structural barriers confront women than men in their attempts to acquire civilized status.

Thus, although both dual-sex and single-sex systems are gender-sensitive, gender operates differently in conjunction with different prestige structures. Civilization means different things, in practice, to men and women, but categories of civilized man and civilized woman are not posited in opposition to each other. Rather, for both sexes, civilized is posited in opposition to native and subsumes gender within this dichotomy. The category "civilized woman" appears to be constructed in opposition to the category "native woman," particularly in regard to criteria of work and productivity. Yet women, unlike men, can slip from civilized to native status by engaging in the "wrong" type of work. This suggests that, contrary to the concept of civilization as introduced by Westerners, the Glebo may be merging this area of prestige with gender to the point of constructing it differently for women than for men, but without separate routes of access or separate sets of positions. The numerous inconsistencies and ambiguities in the application of terms like *civilized* and *native*, which have been discussed throughout this study, testify to the uneasy fit between dual-sex and single-sex systems of prestige.

The Glebo have inserted gender into the civilized/native dichotomy to the point that women's status is not only more tenuous and vulnerable than men's but also very difficult to maintain without male support. There are few independent sources of female prestige in the civilized world, where women may fill roles such as worker, citizen, and so on, but where none of these roles are exclusively for women. As civilized wives of ambitious men, women receive only derivative status from the complementary roles they are expected to fulfill. In addition, such men often find it profitable (and acceptable) to marry additional *lappa* wives, who will add children to the family and support themselves from the farms or the market. These women's roles complement each other, with the civilized wife training the children of rice farmers and marketeers as well as her own. Both complementarities are based on asymmetrical assignments of prestige; the husband is ranked over the wife and the civilized woman over the native women. But the native woman has a series of other statuses open to her within the dual-sex system; the civilized woman's complementary role vis-à-vis her husband is neither named nor recognized by the larger

[169]

system. Hanna Papanek has characterized this female contribution to a husband's status as a "process of 'covert integration' by which it is utilized in the earner's work process but remains unacknowledged and unrewarded in any direct sense" (1979:777).

What, then, may be said about the three related issues posed at the beginning of this book: the intersection of gender and other forms of prestige, the constraining nature of these prestige categories (including gender), and the differential impact of prestige distinctions on women and men? It is clear that gender conditions the attribution of civilized status to different categories of persons; a man with four or five years of formal education who is employed as a storeboy may well be considered civilized while a market woman with an equal amount of schooling is not. The constraining nature of both gender and the civilized/native dichotomy appears most severe in the lives of civilized women, forcing them into economic dependence on men or on close relatives and resulting in such involuted strategies as the alternate marketing system discussed in Chapter 5. The great value and prestige associated with civilization also channel the aspirations of market women and some women farmers for their children, hoping to give them a better and easier life while at the same time placing limits on their future options (especially those of their daughters). Finally, at least some of the differential impact of the civilized/native dichotomy on men and women may be attributed to the contradictions arising from the uneasy combination of a dual-sex with a single-sex system of prestige. As mentioned earlier, the cultural construction of woman as family provider is often invoked against civilized women when they attempt to solicit economic support from the fathers of their children.

The next step in this research would be to go beyond local issues of the Cape Palmas Glebo and examine the larger economic history of Liberia and West Africa in general. The goal would be to understand how the external economic system has created such intermediate categories as that occupied by the market women and the similarly uneducated men who are marginally employed or unemployed. With the bureaucratic sector under pressure from the massive government wage bill and little or no industry to absorb a population unwilling to pursue subsistence farming, a new class system may be emerging in Liberia. I have argued thus far that the civilized/native dichotomy was not originally and is not now a description of class relations, at least among the Glebo. It may be, however, that this situation is in the process of being radically changed.

Is it enough to say that the civilized/native dichotomy is simply a marker of prestige, not of political and economic power? On the local level, as I have argued, I believe this to be the case, but as Pierre Bourdieu suggests, the very existence of such a "distinction" points to relations of domination: "Principles of division, inextricably logical and sociological, function within and for the purposes of the struggle between social groups . . . what is at stake in the struggles about the meaning of the social world is power over the classificatory schemes and systems that are the basis of the representations of groups and therefore of their mobilization and demobilization . . . a separative power, a distinction . . . drawing discrete units out of indivisible continuity, difference out of the undifferentiated" (1984:479).

I am suggesting that to understand Glebo conceptions in light of Bourdieu's warning that distinction always signals domination, we must locate them within the national Liberian political culture. Although the civilized/native distinction may not describe power relations as these are played out in everyday life in Hoffman Station, it clearly did so nationally, at least until recently. From the time of initial settlement until the military coup in 1980, the Liberian repatriate elite defined and exemplified the national ideal of civilization. For this repatriate group, the emergence of educated "civilized natives" represented both a political challenge and a dangerous conflation of categories. The military coup, led by young, noncommissioned officers and enlisted men of indigenous background, was widely seen as the triumph of civilized natives over the repatriate elite and has to some degree brought the national ideology more into line with that held by the Glebo. Criticism of President Samuel K. Doe, who has an eleventh grade education, often centers around his being too "country" for national leadership and echoes the Glebo notion of civilization as contingent on a constellation of factors and practices, not unambiguously based on descent, as in the repatriate ideology (Liberty 1986:45–46). With the

[171]

withdrawal of the repatriate elite from at least the topmost government positions, access to power in the Liberian state is beginning to reflect ethnic competition rather than the civilized/native contrast. On the local level and within ethnic groups, however, these definitions of personal status remain salient.

The Glebo definition of civilization as located in housekeeping and domestic order may be seen as an example of what Bourdieu has called "class habitus" or "embodied class" (1984:473):

> The habitus integrates into the biographically synthesizing unity of a generative principle the set of effects of the determinations imposed by the material conditions of existence (whose efficacy is more or less subordinated to the effects of the training previously undergone as one advances in time). It is embodied class (including biological properties that are socially shaped, such as sex or age) and . . . it is distinguished (in its effects) from class as objectified at a given moment (in the form of property, titles, etc.) inasmuch as it perpetuates a different state of the material conditions of existence—those which produced it and which in this case differ to some extent from the conditions of its operation.

The class habitus of civilized Glebo housekeeping, therefore, is a reflection not of real or "objectified" class differences between them and their native neighbors and kin. Rather than a mirror of local social structural order, it preserves the reflection of an older national power distinction which is rapidly giving way to one based on ethnicity. As a classification system, however, its local-level efficacy is in no way diminished by the shift in national political realities. Any "distinctions" that can assign full siblings to different prestige categories in what is still primarily a kin-based society remains a power to be reckoned with.

Long before Bourdieu considered these problems, Weber had distinguished "social honor" from class by noting that the former may be the basis of both political and economic power, but not vice versa: "Social honor need not necessarily be linked to a 'class situation.' On the contrary, it normally stands in sharp opposition to the pretensions of sheer property. Both propertied and propertyless people can belong to the same status group, and frequently they do with very tangible consequences" (1946:180, 187).

But as we have seen, propertyless women may be denied membership in the civilized status group where propertyless men are not. Furthermore, as the economic climate worsens, the distinctions of wealth between employed professionals and slightly less-educated or well-employed people are likely to become more starkly obvious. The civilized category could potentially develop a recognized internal stratification system of its own, as could the previously unrecognized category of native, unskilled, urban dwellers immediately below it. A possible outcome of such an emerging hierarchy might be the clustering of women in the lower status and economic levels, analogous to the "feminization of poverty" we are witnessing in the United States today.

In any case, it seems evident that any national, regional, or international analysis of both social and economic stratification must begin from the premise that such supposedly gender-neutral terms as "civilization" or even "class" may in fact be highly gender-sensitive. Only then can we achieve a reliable understanding of the impact of change on all those whose lives are affected by it.

Glossary

blo nyene "women's chief," elected female official who speaks for the women of a Glebo town and is recognized as their leader. Highest female secular authority.

bodio "high priest" or chief male ritual authority in a cluster of Glebo towns. See also *gyide*.

dako loose political affiliation of towns recognizing a common origin and obligations for mutual defense. A named identity each Glebo individual acquires patrilineally. Plural: *dakwe*.

dio "country doctor" or indigenous ritual and medical specialist. Plural: *diobo*.

doklo men's "war dance" now performed on the occasion of the funeral or "false burial" of an adult man.

dum kae "mourning house" or house where a death has recently taken place. Also *dum kor*, "mourning mat," mat on the floor where the female relatives of the deceased gather to cry.

gbudubo council of elders, made up of the oldest man in each patriclan in a Glebo town and the oldest woman (by patrifiliation or by marriage) in each clan. Also constitutes the last grade of the men's age-grade system. The council advises the *wodo baa*, or town chief, and meets in the town's ritual center, the *takae*, by which name it is also known.

glorro singing and dancing club for young people.

gyide "high priest's wife," wife of the *bodio* and the highest female ritual authority in a Glebo town.

gyudu "trial by ordeal" in which the accused drinks a decoction of "sassywood" and, if innocent, vomits the mixture. If guilty, the accused dies of its poisonous effects.

kaebuo "house father," the male head of a household.

kaede "house mother," the female head of a household. In polygynous households, the head wife.

kumli burial society that provides an elaborate funeral for its members upon death. From the English word "company."

[175]

Glossary

Kuniwe	a section of the "seaside" Glebo, considered a separate *dako*. Consists of those towns tracing their origin from the ritual center of Taake.
kwi	Civilized, western, or modern. A word of Kru origin which has entered Liberian English.
lappa	a two-yard length of cloth worn around the waist by both men and women. Has become associated with native women and market women.
maasan	female official who leads the women's dancing.
mesa	Indicates civilized status. From the English word "mission."
nana	women's "war dance" performed on the occasion of the death of an elder woman.
Nyomowe	a section of the "seaside" Glebo, considered a separate *dako*. Consists of those towns tracing their origin from the original landing place of Gbenelu.
pano	a named patrilineal clan. *Pane* (plural) cross town, *dako*, and even language lines. Some Kru *panton* have the same names as Glebo *pane*, and their members consider themselves "one family."
sidibo	"soldiers," the age grade of adult married men who in former times had primary responsibility for the defense of the town.
takae	ritual structure that is the home of the *bodio* and *gyide* and the meeting place of the *gbudubo*, which is also known by this name. Usually surrounded by a fence.
tibawa	male official who is the "speaker" for the *sidibo* age grade. Responsible for going last into battle and organizing retreats, if necessary. Also had ritual duties related to success in warfare.
wodo	town, named locality in which it is possible to have patrilineally ascribed rights and obligations.
wodo baa	"town's namesake," the highest secular male authority. Now merged with Liberian government position of town chief. Plural: *wodo baabo*.
yibadio	literally "face eater," male official who in former times led the *sidibo* into battle and who now leads men's funeral dancing. Also had ritual duties related to warfare.

Bibliography

Ajayi, J. F. A., and Michael Crowder, eds. 1974. *History of West Africa*. Vol. 2. London: Longman.

Akpan, M. B. 1973. "Black Imperialism: Americo-Liberian Rule over the African Peoples of Liberia, 1841–1964." *Canadian Journal of African Studies* 7:217–36.

———. 1980. "The Practice of Indirect Rule in Liberia: The Laying of the Foundations, 1822–1915." In Eckhard Hinzen and Robert Kappel, eds., *Dependence, Underdevelopment, and Persistent Conflict: On the Political Economy of Liberia*, pp. 57–168. Bremen: Übersee Museum.

Ardener, Shirley. 1975. "Sexual Insult and Female Militancy." In Shirley Ardener, ed., *Perceiving Women*, pp. 29–53. New York: Wiley.

Azevedo, Warren L. d'. 1962. "Some Historical Problems in the Delineation of a Central West Atlantic Region." *Annals of the New York Academy of Sciences* 96:512–38.

Banton, Michael. 1957. *West African City*. London: Oxford University Press.

Berman, Edward H., ed. 1975. *African Reactions to Missionary Education*. New York: Teacher's College Press.

Bindels, J. A., and H. J. K. Goe. 1983. "Maryland County: Baseline Survey, 1982." Mimeograph. United Nations Development Programme/Self Help Village Development Project in Eastern Liberia. Harper, Maryland County, Liberia.

Bledsoe, Caroline. 1980. *Women and Marriage in Kpelle Society*. Stanford, Calif.: Stanford University Press.

Boahen, Adu. 1974. "Politics in Ghana, 1800–1874." In J. F. A. Ajayi and Michael Crowder, eds., *History of West Africa*, 2:167–261. London: Longman.

Boserup, Esther. 1970. *Woman's Role in Economic Development*. New York: St. Martin's Press.

Bourdieu, Pierre. 1984. *Distinction: A Social Critique of the Judgement of*

Taste. Translated by Richard Nice. Cambridge, Mass.: Harvard University Press.

Bourque, Susan C., and Kay B. Warren. 1981. *Women of the Andes: Patriarchy and Social Change in Two Peruvian Towns.* Ann Arbor: University of Michigan Press.

Brooks, George E. 1962. "A Salem Merchant at Cape Palmas, Liberia, in 1840." *Essex Institute Historical Collections* 98:161–74.

——. 1972. *The Kru Mariner in the Nineteenth Century.* Liberian Studies Monograph Series, No. 1. Newark, Del.: Liberian Studies Association.

Brown, David. 1982. "On the Category 'Civilised' in Liberia and Elsewhere." *Journal of Modern African Studies* 20:287–303.

Brown, Judith K. 1970. "A Note on the Division of Labor by Sex." *American Anthropologist* 72:1073–78.

Buelow, George. 1980–81. "Eve's Rib: Association Membership and Mental Health among Kru Women." *Liberian Studies Journal* 9:23–33.

Carlsson, Jerker. 1980. "The Iron Ore Mining Industry in Liberia: Surplus Generation and Linkages." In Eckhard Hinzen and Robert Kappel, eds., *Dependence, Underdevelopment, and Persistent Conflict: On the Political Economy of Liberia,* pp. 267–94. Bremen: Übersee Museum.

Carter, Jeanette, and Joyce Mends-Cole. 1982. *Liberian Women: Their Role in Food Production and Their Educational and Legal Status.* Monrovia: U.S. AID/University of Liberia, Profile of Liberian Women in Development Project.

Chodorow, Nancy. 1974. "Family Structure and Feminine Personality." In Michelle Rosaldo and Louise Lamphere, eds., *Woman, Culture, and Society,* pp. 43–66. Stanford, Calif.: Stanford University Press.

Clower, Robert W., George Dalton, Mitchell Harwitz, and A. A. Walters. 1966. *Growth without Development: An Economic Survey of Liberia.* Evanston, Ill.: Northwestern University Press.

Cohen, Abner. 1969. *Custom and Politics in Urban Africa.* London: Routledge & Kegan Paul.

——. 1981. *The Politics of Elite Culture.* Berkeley and Los Angeles: University of California Press.

Collier, Jane, and Michelle Rosaldo. 1981. "Politics and Gender in Simple Societies." In Sherry B. Ortner and Harriet Whitehead, eds., *Sexual Meanings: The Cultural Construction of Gender and Sexuality,* pp. 275–329. Cambridge: Cambridge University Press.

Comaroff, John. 1980. "Bridewealth and the Control of Ambiguity in a Tswana Chiefdom." In Comaroff, ed., *The Meaning of Marriage Payments,* pp. 161–96. London: Academic Press.

Conteh, Al-Hassan, S. Momolu Getaweh, and Thomas B. Ken. 1982. "A Study of Three Markets in Monrovia." Mimeograph. Monrovia: Institute of Research, University of Liberia.

Cott, Nancy. 1977. *The Bonds of Womanhood: "Women's Sphere" in New England, 1780–1835.* New Haven: Yale University Press.

Currens, G. E. 1976. "Women, Men, and Rice: Agricultural Innovation in Northwestern Liberia." *Human Organization* 35:355–65.

Danforth, Loring M. 1982. *Death Rituals of Rural Greece*. Princeton, N.J.: Princeton University Press.

Davis, Ronald W. 1968. "Historical Outline of the Kru Coast, 1500 to the Present." Ph.D. dissertation, Indiana University.

Douglas, Mary. 1966. *Purity and Danger: An Analysis of the Concepts of Pollution and Taboo*. London: Routledge & Kegan Paul.

Duitsman, John. 1982–83. "Liberian Languages." *Liberian Studies Journal* 10:27–36.

Dunn, D. Elwood, and S. Byron Tarr. 1988. *Liberia: A National Polity in Transition*. Metuchen, N.J.: Scarecrow Press.

Earp, Charles. 1941. "The Role of Education in the Maryland Colonization Movement." *Journal of Negro History* 26:365–88.

Fortes, Meyer, and E. E. Evans-Pritchard. 1962. *African Political Systems*. London: Oxford University Press.

Fox, George T. 1868. *A Memoir of the Rev. C. Colden Hoffman, Missionary to Cape Palmas, West Africa*. New York: A. D. F. Randolph.

Fraenkel, Merran. 1964. *Tribe and Class in Monrovia*. London: Oxford University Press.

———. 1966. "Social Change on the Kru Coast of Liberia." *Africa* 36:154–72.

Frykman, Jonas, and Orvar Lofgren. 1987. *Culture Builders: A Historical Anthropology of Middle-Class Life*. New Brunswick, N.J.: Rutgers University Press.

Geertz, Clifford. 1965. *The Social History of an Indonesian Town*. Cambridge: MIT Press.

Gershoni, Yekutiel. 1985. *Black Colonialism: The Americo-Liberian Scramble for the Hinterland*. Boulder, Colo.: Westview Press.

Goodale, Jane. 1971. *Tiwi Wives*. Seattle: University of Washington Press.

Green, Margaret M. 1947. *Igbo Village Affairs*. London: Sidgwick & Jackson.

Greenberg, Joseph H. 1963. "The Languages of Africa." *International Journal of American Linguistics* 29:1–171.

Hafkin, Nancy J., and Edna G. Bay. 1976. *Women in Africa: Studies in Social and Economic Change*. Stanford, Calif.: Stanford University Press.

Hair, P. E. H. 1967. "Ethnolinguistic Continuity on the Guinea Coast." *Journal of African History* 8:247–68.

Hanwerker, W. Penn. 1973. "Kinship, Friendship, and Business Failure among Market Sellers in Monrovia, Liberia, 1970." *Africa* 43:288–301.

———. 1974. "Changing Household Organization in the Origins of Market Places in Liberia." *Economic Development and Cultural Change* 22:229–48.

———. 1979. "Daily Markets and Urban Economic Development." *Human Organization* 38:366–76.

———. 1983. "'Natural Fertility' as a Balance of Choice and Behavioral Effect: Policy Implications for Liberian Farm Households." Unpublished paper.

Hasselman, Karl H. 1979. *Liberia: Geographical Mosaics of the Land and the People.* Monrovia: Ministry of Information, Cultural Affairs, and Tourism.

Herzog, George, and Charles Blooah. 1936. *Jabo Proverbs from Liberia.* London: Oxford University Press.

Hill, Polly. 1969. "Hidden Trade in Hausaland." *Man* 4:392–409.

Hinzen, Eckhard, and Robert Kappel. 1980. *Dependence, Underdevelopment, and Persistent Conflict: On the Political Economy of Liberia.* Bremen: Übersee Museum.

Innes, Gordon. 1966. *An Introduction to Grebo.* London: School of Oriental and African Studies.

———. 1967. *A Grebo-English Dictionary.* London: Cambridge University Press.

Johnson, S. Jangaba M. 1957. *Traditional History and Folklore of the Glebo Tribe.* Monrovia: Bureau of Folkways, Republic of Liberia.

Johnston, Sir Harry. 1906. *Liberia.* 2 vols. London: Hutchinson.

Jones, Abeodu Bowen. 1974. "The Republic of Liberia." In J. F. A. Ajayi and Michael Crowder, eds., *History of West Africa*, 2:308–43. London: Longman.

Kaba, Brahima D., Joyce O. Smith, J. Boley Dovee, and Aminata W. Conteh. 1982. *Liberian Women in the Marketplace.* Monrovia: U.S. AID/University of Liberia, Profile of Liberian Women in Development Project.

Kappel, Robert. 1980. "Resistance of the Liberian Peoples: Problems of the Ignored Facts." In Eckhard Hinzen and Robert Kappel, eds., *Dependence, Underdevelopment, and Persistent Conflict: On the Political Economy of Liberia*, pp. 169–96. Bremen: Übersee Museum.

Kirkpatrick, John. 1980. "Are Male and Female Genders in the Marquesas?" Paper presented at the Annual Meeting of the American Anthropological Association, Washington, D.C.

Lancaster, Chet S. 1976. "Women, Horticulture and Society in Sub-Saharan Africa." *American Anthropologist* 78:539–64.

Latrobe, John H. B. 1885. "Maryland in Liberia: A Paper Read before the Maryland Historical Society." *Maryland Historical Society Fund Publications* 21:7–134.

Leacock, Eleanor. 1978. "Women's Status in Egalitarian Society: Implications for Social Evolution." *Current Anthropology* 19:247–75.

Lebeuf, Annie M. D. 1963. "The Role of Women in the Political Organization of African Societies." In Denise Paulme, ed., *Women of Tropical Africa*, pp. 93–120. Berkeley and Los Angeles: University of California Press.

Leith-Ross, Sylvia. 1939. *African Women: A Study of the Ibo of Nigeria.* London: Faber & Faber.

Lévi-Strauss, Claude. 1969. *The Elementary Structures of Kinship.* Translated by James Harle Bell, John Richard von Sturmer, and Rodney Needham. Boston: Beacon Press.

Liberia, Republic of. 1976. *Census of Population and Housing.* Bulletin No. 2. Monrovia: Ministry of Planning and Economic Affairs.

Liberty, C. E. Zamba. 1986. "Report from Musardu (Letter to an American Friend): Reflections on the Liberian Crisis." *Liberian Studies Journal* 11:42–81.

Liebenow, J. Gus. 1969. *Liberia: The Evolution of Privilege.* Ithaca, N.Y.: Cornell University Press.

———. 1987. *Liberia: The Quest for Democracy.* Bloomington: Indiana University Press.

Linton, Ralph. 1936. *The Study of Man.* New York: D. Appleton.

Little, Kenneth. 1966. *West African Urbanization.* Cambridge: Cambridge University Press.

———. 1973. *African Women in Towns.* Cambridge: Cambridge University Press.

McEvoy, Frederick D. 1971. "History, Tradition and Kinship as Factors in Modern Sabo Labor Migration." Ph.D. dissertation, University of Oregon.

———. 1977. "Understanding Ethnic Realities among the Grebo and Kru Peoples of West Africa." *Africa* 47:62–79.

Martin, Jane Jackson. 1968. "The Dual Legacy: Government Authority and Mission Influence among the Glebo of Eastern Liberia, 1834–1910." Ph.D. dissertation, Boston University.

———. 1982. "Krumen 'Down the Coast': Liberian Migrants on the West African Coast in the Nineteenth Century." Boston University African Studies Center Working Papers, No. 64.

Mead, Margaret. 1935. *Sex and Temperament in Three Primitive Societies.* New York: Dell.

Mintz, Sidney. 1971. "Men, Women, and Trade." *Comparative Studies in Society and History* 13:247–69.

Moran, Mary H. 1985. "'Civilized Women': Gender and Prestige among the Glebo of Cape Palmas, Liberia." Ph.D. dissertation, Brown University.

———. 1986. "Taking Up the Slack: Female Farming and the 'Kru Problem' in Southeastern Liberia." *Liberian Studies Journal* 11:117–24.

———. 1989. "Collective Action and the 'Representation' of African Women: A Liberian Case Study." *Feminist Studies*, forthcoming.

Murdock, George P. 1959. *Africa: Its Peoples and Their Culture History.* New York: McGraw-Hill.

Okonjo, Kamene. 1976. "The Dual-Sex Political System in Operation: Igbo Women and Community Politics in Midwestern Nigeria." In Nancy J. Hafkin and Edna G. Bay, eds., *Women in Africa: Studies in Social*

[181]

and Economic Change, pp. 45–58. Stanford, Calif.: Stanford University Press.

Ortner, Sherry B. 1974. "Is Female to Male as Nature is to Culture?" In Michelle Rosaldo and Louise Lamphere, eds., *Woman, Culture, and Society*, pp. 67–87. Stanford, Calif.: Stanford University Press.

——. 1984. "Theory in Anthropology since the Sixties." *Comparative Studies in Society and History* 26:126–66.

Ortner, Sherry B., and Harriet Whitehead, eds. 1981. *Sexual Meanings: The Cultural Construction of Gender and Sexuality*. Cambridge: Cambridge University Press.

Ottenberg, Phoebe. 1959. "The Changing Economic Position of Women among the Afikpo Ibo." In William Bascom and Melville J. Herskovits, eds., *Continuity and Change in African Cultures*, pp. 205–23. Chicago: University of Chicago Press.

Papanek, Hanna. 1979. "Family Status Production: The 'Work' and 'Non-Work' of Women." *Signs* 4:775–81.

Paulme, Denise, ed. 1963. *Women of Tropical Africa*. Berkeley and Los Angeles: University of California Press.

Payne, John. 1845. "The Journal of the Rev. John Payne." *Spirit of the Missions* 10:113–45, 241–303, 330–65, 395.

Radke, Johannes, and Peter Sauer. 1980. "The Influence of the Colonial Powers in Liberia before the First World War." In Eckhard Hinzen and Robert Kappel, eds., *Dependence, Underdevelopment, and Persistent Conflict: On the Political Economy of Liberia*, pp. 11–56. Bremen: Übersee Museum.

Remy, Dorothy. 1975. "Underdevelopment and the Experience of Women: A Nigerian Case Study." In Rayna R. Reiter, ed., *Toward an Anthropology of Women*, pp. 358–71. New York: Monthly Review Press.

Rogers, Susan C. 1978. "Women's Place: A Critical Review of Anthropological Theory." *Comparative Studies in Society and History* 20:123–62.

Rosaldo, Michelle. 1974. "Woman, Culture, and Society: A Theoretical Overview." In Michelle Rosaldo and Louise Lamphere, eds., *Woman, Culture, and Society*, pp. 17–42. Stanford, Calif.: Stanford University Press.

——. 1980. "The Use and Abuse of Anthropology: Reflections on Feminism and Cross-Cultural Understanding." *Signs* 5:389–417.

Rosaldo, Michelle, and Louise Lamphere, eds. 1974. *Woman, Culture, and Society*. Stanford, Calif.: Stanford University Press.

Rubin, Gayle. 1975. "The Traffic in Women: Notes on the 'Political Economy' of Sex." In Rayna R. Reiter, ed., *Toward an Anthropology of Women*, pp. 157–210. New York: Monthly Review Press.

Ryan, Mary P. 1981. *Cradle of the Middle Class: The Family in Oneida County, New York*. New York: Cambridge University Press.

Sacks, Karen. 1979. *Sisters and Wives: The Past and Future of Sexual Equality.* Westport, Conn.: Greenwood Press.

Schmokel, W. W. 1969. "Settlers and Tribes: The Origins of the Liberian Dilemma." In Daniel McCall, Norman Bennett, and Jeffery Butler, eds., *Western African History,* pp. 153–73. Boston University Papers on Africa, Vol. 4. New York: Praeger.

Schulze, Willi. 1973. *A New Geography of Liberia.* London: Longman.

Schwab, George. 1947. "Tribes of the Liberian Hinterland." *Harvard University Peabody Museum Papers,* vol. 31.

Smith, Mary F. 1981. *Baba of Karo: A Woman of the Muslim Hausa.* New Haven: Yale University Press.

Staudenraus, P. J. 1961. *The African Colonization Movement, 1816–1865.* New York: Columbia University Press.

Strathern, Marilyn. 1981. "Self-Interest and Social Good: Some Implications of Hagen Gender Imagery." In Sherry B. Ortner and Harriet Whitehead, eds., *Sexual Meanings: The Cultural Construction of Gender and Sexuality,* pp. 166–91. Cambridge: Cambridge University Press.

Sullivan, Jo Mary. 1978. "Settlers in Sinoe County, Liberia, and Their Relations with the Kru, c. 1835–1920." Ph.D. dissertation, Boston University.

Sundiata, I. K. 1980. *Black Scandal: America and the Liberian Labor Crisis, 1929–1936.* Philadelphia: Institute for the Study of Human Issues.

Tonkin, Elizabeth. 1978–79. "Sasstown's Transformation: The Jlao Kru, 1888–1918." *Liberian Studies Journal* 8:1–34.

———. 1980. "Jealousy Names, Civilised Names: Anthroponomy of the Jlao Kru of Liberia." *Man* 15:653–64.

———. 1981. "Model and Ideology: Dimensions of Being Civilised in Liberia." In Ladislav Holy and Milan Stuchlik, eds., *The Structure of Folk Models,* pp. 305–30. London: Academic Press.

Turner, Victor. 1969. *The Ritual Process.* Ithaca, N.Y.: Cornell University Press.

Van Allen, Judith. 1972. "Sitting on a Man: Colonialism and the Lost Political Institutions of Igbo Women." *Canadian Journal of African Studies* 6:165–81.

———. 1976. "Aba Riots or Igbo Women's War? Ideology, Stratification, and the Invisibility of Women." In Nancy J. Hafkin and Edna G. Bay, eds., *Women in Africa: Studies in Social and Economic Change;* pp. 59–86. Stanford, Calif.: Stanford University Press.

van der Kraaij, Fred. 1980. "Firestone in Liberia." In Eckhard Hinzen and Robert Kappel, eds., *Dependence, Underdevelopment, and Persistent Conflict: On the Political Economy of Liberia,* pp. 199–266. Bremen: Übersee Museum.

Vincent, Joan. 1968. *African Elite: The Big Men of a Small Town*. New York: Columbia University Press.

Wallace, Samuel Yede. 1955. *Historical Lights of Gedebo or Glebo (Yesterday and Today Glebo)*. Harper City, Cape Palmas, Liberia: Published by the Author.

———. 1980. "The Complete History of Yesterday and Today Grebo." Unpublished Ms.

———. 1983. "The Autobiography of Samuel Yede Wallace." Unpublished Ms.

Warren, Kay B. 1983. "When Cosmologies Lie: Gender, Politics, and Value in the Andes." Paper presented at the Pembroke Center for Research and Teaching on Women, Brown University.

Weber, Max. 1946. *From Max Weber: Essays in Sociology*. Ed. Hans H. Gerth and C. Wright Mills. New York: Oxford University Press.

———. 1947. *The Theory of Social and Economic Organization*. Ed. Talcott Parsons. New York: Oxford University Press.

Weiner, Annette B. 1976. *Women of Value, Men of Renown: New Perspectives in Trobriand Exchange*. Austin: University Of Texas Press.

White, E. Frances. 1987. *Sierra Leone's Settler Women Traders: Women on the Afro-European Frontier.* Ann Arbor: University of Michigan Press.

Whitehead, Harriet. 1981. "The Bow and the Burden Strap: A New Look at Institutionalized Homosexuality in Native North America." In Sherry B. Ortner and Harriet Whitehead, eds., *Sexual Meanings: The Cultural Construction of Gender and Sexuality*, pp. 80–115. Cambridge: Cambridge University Press.

Wilson, J. L. 1856. *Western Africa*. New York: Harper & Brothers.

Wolf, Margery. 1972. *Women and the Family in Rural Taiwan*. Stanford, Calif.: Stanford University Press.

Index

Index

Collier, Jane, 12
Colonization movement, 44–47. *See also*
    African-Americans; Repatriates;
    Settlers
Conteh, Al-Hassan, 118–19, 125
Cott, Nancy, 67
Credit, 122–23, 131, 133–34, 161, 163
Currens, G. E., 111, 113

Dako, 18–22, 111; and identity, 22–23,
    32, 35, 107, 137–38
Danforth, Loring M., 148
Davis, Ronald, 15, 43
Death, 24, 29, 37–39, 69, 137, 142–43,
    148–65. *See also* Funerals; Wakes
Demography. *See* Towns: demography of
Divorce, 24, 69, 120
Domesticity, 4–5, 64–68, 92, 100, 102,
    125, 134, 172–73. *See also* Households
Douglas, Mary, 67
Dual administration, 61–62, 80, 84, 86.
    See also Political organization
Dunn, D. Elwood, 58, 59

Earp, Charles, 46, 53, 54
Education: and civilized status, 3, 5, 12,
    43–44, 46, 50–56, 59, 63–66, 87–88,
    91–92, 100–102, 106–8, 134–36, 167–
    68, 170; cost of, 4, 91, 101, 122, 124,
    137; in Harper area, 66–67, 81, 82,
    87, 90–91, 141; and missions, 46, 52–
    56, 60–63, 141; of women, 4, 52, 67,
    71, 107, 112, 118, 126–27, 135
Employment: and civilized status, 5, 44,
    53, 63–64, 66, 69–70, 94–97, 126; on
    foreign concessions, 49–51; in Harper
    area, 2, 4, 7, 55, 61, 66, 70, 94–97,
    102, 120–21, 136; of household heads,
    97–99; on Kru Coast, 62, 69–70. *See
    also* Work
England, 48–50, 56–58, 62
Episcopal Church, 44, 47, 51–56, 69, 77,
    79, 135, 140–41, 143, 147, 154, 156,
    164. *See also* Missionaries; St. James
    Church
Episcopal Church Women, 143, 147,
    158, 161
Ethnic Diversity, 64, 76–77, 83, 108,
    116, 172
Ethnicity: and group identity, 21–22, 56,
    60, 63; and language, 15, 17–18; and
    Liberian state, 21, 63, 172
Evans-Pritchard, E. E., 166

Farming, 3, 7, 8, 20–21, 28, 70, 94–95,
    100, 102–3, 109, 111, 121, 128; and
    cash crops, 112–13; subsistence, 5,
    50–51, 53, 107, 110–13, 118–19, 127–
    28, 170
Female farmers, 13, 28, 108–9, 111–13,
    118, 121, 127–28, 133, 169. *See also*
    Native women
Firestone, Harvey, 49–50
Firestone Rubber Company, 49–51
Foreign investment, 49–51, 62
Fortes, Meyer, 166
Fosterage, 8, 13, 66, 73, 86–92, 100–
    102, 107–9, 120, 129, 131, 134, 136–
    38, 156. *See also* Servants
Fox, George, T., 46, 52, 54
Fraenkel, Merran, 1, 2, 43, 60–65, 80,
    86, 91, 94, 138, 146, 161
Free people of color, 44–46
Frykman, Jonas, 67
Funerals, 8–9, 13, 78, 103, 130, 139,
    144–45, 148, 150, 152, 157–65; Chris-
    tian, 142–43, 152, 157, 164; dancing
    at, 29, 33, 82, 86, 112, 145, 149–50,
    153–54, 159–61

Gbarnga, 118–20, 123, 125, 127, 134
Gbede, 20, 21, 27, 47, 52, 54, 85, 103
Gbenelu, 18, 20–21, 31–32, 45, 47, 55,
    73, 76–78, 80–87, 91–95, 97–98, 100,
    102–3, 105, 108, 118, 120, 132, 138–
    39, 141, 144, 146, 149, 161, 163
Geertz, Clifford, 10–11
Gender: and age, 30; and asymmetry, 9–
    12, 30, 167–68; cultural constructions
    of, 5, 9, 24, 27–29, 31, 52, 56, 66, 69–
    71, 98, 109, 128, 166; as prestige
    structure, 11–12, 27, 71–72, 166–73;
    theories of, 8–13
Gershoni, Yekutiel, 48
Grand Cess, 60, 62, 65, 86, 94, 138, 146
Grebo languages, 2, 15–18, 21–22, 24,
    43, 52, 78, 81, 115–17
Green, Margaret, 166
Greenberg, Joseph H., 15

Hafkin, Nancy, 166
Hair, P. E. H., 42
Handwerker, W. Penn, 87, 109, 114,
    126–27, 133
Harper, 47–48, 51–53, 55, 60–66, 74–
    78, 80–82, 84, 85, 91–92, 94, 96–97,
    101–4, 108, 113–15, 118–23, 125–26,

Library of Congress Cataloging-in-Publication Data

Moran, Mary H., 1957–
  Civilized women.
  (Anthropology of contemporary issues)
  Includes bibliographical references.
  1. Women, Grebo (African people)—Social conditions. 2. Women, Grebo
(African people)—Economic conditions. 3. Harper (Liberia)—Social
conditions. 4. Harper (Liberia)—Economic conditions. I. Title. II. Series.
DT630.5.G6M67 1990 306'.089963306662 89-22398
  ISBN 0-8014-2293-0 (alk. paper)
  ISBN 0-8014-9554-7 (pbk. : alk. paper)